THE
BIG
BOOK OF
WOK & STIR FRY

THE BIG BOOK OF WOK & STIR FRY

Your complete guide to successful
stir-fry cooking

Love Food ® is an imprint of Parragon Books Ltd

Parragon
Queen Street House
4 Queen Street
Bath BA1 1HE, UK

Copyright © Parragon Books Ltd 2009

Love Food ® and the accompanying heart device is a trade mark of Parragon Books Ltd

ISBN: 978-1-4075-6442-5

Printed in China

Internal design by Simon Levy
New photography by Charlie Richards
New home economy by Anna Burges-Lumsden, assisted by Mima Sinclair
New recipes, introduction and cover text by Christine McFadden

Notes for the Reader

This book uses both metric and imperial measurements. Follow the same units of measurement throughout; do not mix metric and imperial. All spoon measurements are level: teaspoons are assumed to be 5 ml, and tablespoons are assumed to be 15 ml. Unless otherwise stated, milk is assumed to be full fat, eggs and individual vegetables are medium, and pepper is freshly ground black pepper.

The times given are an approximate guide only. Preparation times differ according to the techniques used by different people and the cooking times may also vary from those given. Optional ingredients, variations or serving suggestions have not been included in the calculations.

Recipes using raw or very lightly cooked eggs should be avoided by infants, the elderly, pregnant women, convalescents and anyone suffering from an illness. Pregnant and breastfeeding women are advised to avoid eating peanuts and peanut products. Sufferers from nut allergies should be aware that some of the ready-made ingredients used in the recipes in this book may contain nuts. Always check the packaging before use.

CONTENTS

INTRODUCTION

The workhorse of the Chinese kitchen, the wok has been in use for over 2000 years. The basic shape remains unchanged, and it is still the essential cooking vessel in the poorest of homes and the most luxurious of restaurants.

Historically, cooking vessels evolved for a number of reasons, a key issue being the type of fuel available. This, in turn, dictated the design and the type of food that could be cooked. In China, fuel was mainly wood, charcoal or animal dung. Supplies were meagre and unpredictable, and much of Chinese cuisine is therefore based on poverty and coping with the harsh conditions commonplace in a predominately agrarian society. The cooking method had to make efficient use of whatever precious fuel was available, and the pan had to heat up quickly. The wok's conical shape and high flaring sides were a masterpiece of design in that respect. Made of metal, it conducted heat quickly, creating a small but intensely hot area at the base. This made it possible for bite-sized morsels of food to be quickly stir-fried using relatively little fuel and cooking oil.

The wok was designed for use over the traditional Chinese pit stove – a charcoal or wood fire set below a rectangular 'fire bench' in which round holes or pits were recessed to hold the wok in place. The wok sat snugly in the holes, the wide flaring sides preventing it from dropping into the fire below. The heat rising from the fuel was fully directed to the bottom of the wok, and no heat escaped round the edges.

Nowadays, pit-style stoves are heated with natural gas, but they follow the same principle with concentrically sloping grates or burners recessed below the stove's surface. The stoves in restaurants and communal kitchens can accommodate gigantic woks for boiling water and cooking huge quantities of rice or soup. At the other end of the scale, the wok may be used over the simplest of braziers, which were, and still are, the mainstay of the kitchen for poverty-stricken families.

MULTI-PURPOSE COOKING VESSEL

Thanks to its unique shape, the wok can cope with virtually all types of food and cooking techniques. Once the base is hot, the heat spreads through the entire inside surface, creating a far greater cooking surface than Western pots and pans with vertical sides. This in turn creates a range of cooking temperatures in one pan – pieces of food that have been seared in the bottom of the wok can be pushed up the sides to continue cooking at a slower rate. Meanwhile, another ingredient for the same dish is added and cooked at high heat in the bottom.

Though most often used for stir-frying, the wok can also be used for steaming, boiling, braising, deep-frying, shallow-frying and smoking.

There are two basic wok designs, the Cantonese and the Pau or Peking, both of which are used throughout China. The Cantonese has two rounded handles that make it easier to use when full of liquid – during steaming or deep-frying, for example. The Pau wok has one long handle and is more convenient, and safer too, for stir-frying. The pan is held in one hand and shaken while the food is turned with a long-handled ladle or spoon held in the other. The long handle distances the cook from the intense heat and hot oil. Some long-handled woks have a small round handle on the opposite side, which comes in handy when carrying the hot wok from stove to table.

MATERIALS

Woks were traditionally made of cast-iron, which maintains a steady even heat. It is worth noting that Chinese cast-iron woks are thinner and lighter than the Western equivalent. They heat up more quickly and also form a more stable layer of seasoning that prevents food from sticking (see Seasoning a wok, page 10). The downside is that they are prone to shattering if mishandled or dropped. Western cast-iron woks, on the other hand, are sturdier but slow to heat up and cool down, making all-important temperature control during stir-frying more difficult.

Currently, the most widely used material is carbon steel. Steel woks are relatively light in weight, conduct heat evenly and are quick to heat up. However, they vary widely in price and quality. The best are made with two sheets of carbon steel that are formed into shape by hand hammering. You can spot them by the small ridges and dimples on the inside of the wok. The lowest quality are stamped from a single sheet of steel and likely to distort after a while.

HEALTH BENEFITS

Thanks to its versatility, the wok can be used for healthy ways of cooking. Stir-frying allows you to enjoy the pleasure of fried food without an unhealthy amount of oil. Unlike a standard frying pan with a wide flat base, the wok requires very little oil to lubricate the food – all that's needed is a tablespoon or so in the base. If you're counting calories, you can even use non-stick cooking spray. Because of the high temperature the food cooks very quickly without soaking up oil. Once cooked, it is pushed up the sloping sides of the wok and the oil drains back to the bottom.

Steaming is another healthy option and is easy to do in a wok (see Basic Techniques, page 12). It is perfect for vegetables and tender items such as fish and chicken. The moist environment means no fat is needed, and fewer nutrients leach into the cooking water since the food does not come in contact with it.

Stewing and braising are also possible in a wok. From a health point of view, fewer nutrients are lost, and fat can be kept to a minimum.

ASIAN CUISINES

Though the wok originated in China, similar cooking vessels are used in East, Southeast and Southern Asia. Depending on the cuisine, they are used in conjunction with other pots and pans, or, as in China's case, they may be the primary cooking vessel.

The shape and name vary depending on country. In Japan the wok is known as a *chukanabe* (literally 'Chinese pot'). It is shallower and flatter, and used like a regular frying pan. The *dare-oh* of Burma is a rounded deep pan similar to a wok. It is made of brass or cast-iron and has a looped handle on either side. The Indonesian *wajan* is deeper with straighter sides, while the Vietnamese *chao* is smaller and shallower. In Malaysia the wok is called a *kuali* (small wok) or *kawa* (big wok). Perhaps the best-known variation is the Indian *karahi*, a type of flat-bottomed wok with two round handles.

Cuisines may vary from country to country and region to region, but many of the basic cooking styles and techniques have their roots in the use of the wok, even though other cooking vessels may be used as well.

CHINA

As vast as the United States, China spans many degrees of latitude, resulting in radical variations in topography and climate. It is this diversity that lies behind intriguing variations in regional cooking.

In Peking in the north, the cooking is homely and robust, famous for lamb and duck as well as roast and barbecued dishes. However, the wok is essential for braising hearty stews, deep-frying whole fish and stir-frying 'seaweed' – a typical dish of the region. The wok is also used for cooking noodles, which are the staple rather than rice.

Canton in the south offers an astonishing melting pot of culinary feasts. The region is renowned for top-notch seafood, fresh fruit and vegetables, and it is here that the wok takes centre stage. The cooks excel at stir-fries and steamed dim sum (stuffed dumplings), and are keen to experiment with ingredients from abroad.

Located around the Yangtze delta in the east, Shanghai cuisine is a mixture of styles, characterized by rich complex flavours and the lavish use of the dark soy sauce for which the delta is renowned. The wok's versatility is ideal for the region's slow-cooked dishes, delicate soups, deep-fried fish and stir-fried rice.

Known as 'the land of plenty', Szechuan (in the west) produces an enormous variety of vegetables, fungi and fish that are put to good use in rich, heavily sauced dishes cooked in the wok. Szechuan is also famous for smoked duck, a three-stage dish cooked entirely in the wok. The duck is first smoked, then steamed to get rid of excess fat, and finally deep-fried until the meat falls apart.

SOUTHEAST ASIA: INDONESIA, MALAYSIA AND THAILAND

As in Chinese cuisine, the wok is a vital piece of kitchen equipment. Without the lid, it is perfect for simmering the region's famous green and red curries; the wide surface allows just the right kind of rapid evaporation needed to reduce the sauce. The initial stir-frying of curry spices also takes place in the wok, where the intense heat at the base quickly brings out their fragrance. With the lid in place, the wok is used for cooking rice by absorption – a method that requires less water and fuel than boiling.

The wok is particularly important in regions of Southeast Asia where fuel is in short supply: the arid north-east of Thailand, for example, where wood is difficult to find, and the central plains which have been cleared of forests and given over to rice paddies. In the well-forested north, however, easy access to fuel allows a greater choice of cooking techniques such as grilling and roasting, or lengthy simmering in enormous cauldrons.

INDIA

Like China, India's vast size and radical variations in topography and climate result in highly regional cuisines. The diversity is most obvious in the contrast between the rich, meat-based dishes of the north and the vegetarian and fish-based cuisine of the south, where rice is the staple food.

The varied cuisine calls for a variety of cooking vessels. These include conventional saucepans and frying pans, as well as the *karahi*, an Indian version of the Chinese wok. It is used for deep-frying or slowly simmering meat, poultry, seafood and pulse dishes. Many Indian homes have two *karahis*: a deep one with a narrow top that is used for deep-frying, and a shallower one with a much wider top that is used for occasional stir-frying, shallow-frying and simmering.

ESSENTIAL EQUIPMENT

You don't need a great deal of specialist equipment to produce authentic Asian-style food, since there is usually an equivalent Western utensil. Useful items are listed below, the most indispensable being a wok and a cleaver.

Wok

The wok's conical shape makes it particularly suitable for stir-frying – the food continually falls to the centre where the heat is most intense, so it cooks in a few minutes. Some woks have a slightly flattened base for use on a ceramic or electric hob. If fitted with a lid and a stand, a wok can also be used for deep-frying, steaming and braising.

Woks come in various sizes and materials. Carbon steel conducts heat evenly and quickly, but needs scrupulous drying to prevent rust, and seasoning to prevent sticking. Cast-iron is also good but it is heavy and, like carbon steel, needs drying and seasoning. Anodized aluminium is reasonably maintenance-free and a good choice for the beginner. Stainless steel looks impressive but food tends to stick and burn, and it is also harder to keep clean.

For family-sized meals, you will need a roomy wok about 35 cm/14 inches wide. A 25-cm/10-inch wok comes in handy for a single serving or stir-frying a few vegetables.

For stir-frying, use a wok with a long wooden handle. Wood will stay cool despite the intense heat of the wok. A hollow metal handle will also remain reasonably cool. Some woks have two round handles instead of a long one. This type may be used for deep-frying, braising and steaming.

Seasoning a wok:

A new steel or iron wok should be scrubbed to get rid of any rust or factory oil. Place it over medium heat to dry. While still hot, smear all over with a wad of kitchen paper soaked in cooking oil. Repeat two or three times using clean paper. Allow to cool, then rinse and dry thoroughly.

Cleaning and maintenance:

Wash with hot water but no detergent as this will remove the seasoned coating. Dry over medium heat. Coat with a thin film of oil to prevent rusting.

Cleaver

A cleaver has a rigid rectangular blade that tapers abruptly to a razor-sharp bevelled edge. It is a multi-purpose tool that may be used to slice, dice, fillet, shred, crush and chop all kinds of food. The back of the blade can be used for pounding, while the flat side comes in handy for transferring ingredients from chopping board to wok.

Cleavers come in different weights, sizes and materials. The heaviest are for chopping bones, while the lighter ones are for slicing meat and fish, and preparing vegetables. Traditional cleavers are made of carbon steel, which is susceptible to rust and will discolor after contact with acidic foods. They need wiping rather than washing and should be given a light coating of vegetable oil to prevent rusting.

The best modern cleavers are made of high-carbon no-stain steel, which is relatively rust-free, and has a superior cutting edge.

Chopping board

It's a good idea to have at least two boards: one for raw poultry, meat and fish, and another for vegetables and herbs. A polyethylene board is best for poultry as it is dishwasher-proof and the heat will sanitize it.

The traditional Chinese chopping board is a thick slab made with a single cross-section of tree trunk. Western boards are made with jointed sections of wood that are prone to splitting and warping. The sturdiest are made with bamboo or a smooth tight-grained hardwood such as maple, beech or cherry. The board should be about 4 cm/1¹/₂ inches thick to absorb the impact of repeated chopping and to resist warping.

Steamer

The traditional Chinese bamboo steamer has gaps in the bamboo that allow excess moisture to escape, preventing the food from becoming waterlogged. Bamboo steamers come in a range of sizes and can be stacked in a wok or pan of boiling water, so you can cook several dishes at the same time.

Ladle

The Chinese use a special ladle for stir-frying. It has a wide shallow bowl that is ideal for lifting, tossing and turning, and an extra-long handle to distance you from the heat. There are also wire mesh ladles for scooping up deep-fried foods. The wire allows oil to drain away quickly.

BASIC TECHNIQUES

Chopping

Cut fresh ingredients into small evenly sized pieces so that they cook in the same amount of time. Slicing meat and vegetables diagonally increases the surface area in contact with the hot oil and speeds up cooking.

Stir-frying

Before you begin, have all the ingredients measured and prepared. The wok must be very hot before you add any oil – hold your hand flat just above the base until you can feel the heat. Using a long-handled ladle or long wooden cooking chopsticks, constantly stir and toss the ingredients so that they all come in contact with the hot oil and are evenly cooked.

Deep-frying

Use enough oil to give a depth of about 5cm. Heat over medium–high heat until a faint haze appears. If the oil is not hot enough, the food will become soggy instead of crisp. Cook in small batches – overcrowding lowers the temperature of the oil and causes uneven cooking. Remove the food with a wire ladle or tongs and drain thoroughly on paper towels.

Braising

Braising is generally used for tougher cuts of meat and dense-fleshed vegetables. The ingredients are briefly stir-fried then simmered in stock until tender.

Steaming

This method is used in China to cook whole fish, dumplings, vegetables and morsels of poultry and meat. The ingredients must be very fresh. Place the food on a heatproof plate or in a perforated container above boiling liquid in the base of a wok. Cover with a lid to trap the steam, which then permeates the food. Depending on size and density, food may be steamed for as little as 10 minutes or up to 2 or 3 hours.

STORE-CUPBOARD INGREDIENTS

You will need basic seasonings, oils and various other store-cupboard items, many of which you will probably already have. Most are easily found in supermarkets, health food shops and Chinese grocers. More obscure items are available by mail order or on-line.

Alcohols for flavouring

Rice wine is widely used in China. It imparts a rich mellow flavour to marinades, stir-fries and braised dishes. A good-quality, pale, dry sherry is a reasonable substitute.

Mirin is a Japanese sweet rice wine. It is used in dressings and marinades, and is an essential ingredient in the sticky brown teriyaki sauce used for glazing grilled meats.

Baby sweetcorn

Available fresh or canned, the cobs have a sweet flavour and an irresistible crunchy texture.

Bamboo shoots

Sold ready-sliced in cans. Once opened, they will keep for up to a week in the refrigerator covered and in fresh water.

Bean sauce

Made from yellow or black fermented soy beans mixed with flour, salt and spices.

Black beans

Small, black, fermented soy beans with a distinctive flavour and aroma.

Dried fungi

Valued for texture as well as flavour, Chinese dried fungi include cloud ears, wood ears, 'black' mushrooms, and shiitake. Straw mushrooms, grown on rice straw, are bite-sized and available canned or dried.

Dried noodles

Noodles are made with different flours: wheat, rice, mung bean and buckwheat. They range from thin round threads to broad flat ribbons. Cook according to the packet instructions as timings vary between brands.

Fish sauce

A watery, brown, salty liquid made with fermented fish with a powerful aroma and flavour. Widely used in Southeast Asia, it imparts a special richness to dishes. The fishy flavour dissipates during cooking. Best bought in small bottles – once opened, it should be used within a few weeks.

Five-spice powder

A Chinese spice blend that includes star anise, cassia, cloves, fennel seeds and Szechuan pepper. Use it sparingly in marinades and sauces. It can be stored in an airtight container for at least a year.

Hoi sin sauce

A thick, brown, sweet and spicy sauce made from fermented soy bean paste, garlic, vinegar, sugar, spices and other flavourings. Used as a dipping sauce with other ingredients, and as a glaze for roasted meat. It can be kept in the refrigerator for months.

Oils

Peanut oil is best for stir-frying and deep-frying. It has a neutral flavour and can be heated to a higher temperature than most oils. Rapeseed and sunflower oils are useful vegetable oils.

Sesame oil has a rich, nutty flavour. A few drops are sprinkled over dishes just before serving. It may also be used sparingly, in combination with groundnut oil, for stir-frying.

Oyster sauce

A thick, brown, richly flavoured sauce popular in southern China. Made with oysters, soy sauce, salt and spices. It has a salty, slightly fishy flavour, which dissipates during cooking. It can be kept in the refrigerator for months.

Rice vinegar

Japanese white rice vinegar is amber-coloured with a clean tart flavour. It is used for flavouring sushi rice. Chinese white rice vinegar is sharper but also good with rice. Chinese brown rice vinegar is fruitier and useful for marinades and dressings. Black rice vinegar is mellow and sweet, and used in slow-cooked caramelised duck or pork dishes.

Sugar

Sugar is used in savoury dishes to balance the saltiness of soy and fish sauce, and the sourness of tamarind. Palm sugar, or jaggery, is used in Southeast Asia. It is sold in compressed brown blocks and has a distinctive caramel flavour.

Soy sauce

A Chinese staple made from fermented soy beans and wheat flour, used both for cooking and at the table. Light soy sauce is more suitable for vegetable, poultry and seafood dishes, soups and dipping sauces. Dark soy sauce is slightly thicker and stronger. It is used in 'red-cooked' stews, and goes well with beef and lamb.

Shoyu is a Japanese soy sauce that is slightly sweeter and less salty than Chinese light soy sauce. Tamari is a rich, dark, Japanese-style sauce, made without wheat.

Szechuan pepper

These are tiny reddish-brown husks from the berries of the prickly ash tree. Widely used in hot and spicy dishes of the Szechuan region in China, the husks are numbing rather than hot, and have a strong lemony flavour.

Tamarind

Made with the pulp extracted from the pods of the tamarind tree. It comes in compressed blocks that are dissolved in hot water, or as a ready-made paste sold in jars. It has a sour lemony flavour.

Tofu (bean curd)

Made with curds from coagulated soy bean milk. The curds are moulded into creamy-white blocks that are compressed until 'silken' or 'firm'. Firm tofu can be sliced into cubes and stir-fried, but needs cooking carefully as it will disintegrate if stirred too much. Tofu can be kept for a few days in the refrigerator if covered with fresh water.

Water chestnuts

Crisp, mildly flavoured tubers available peeled and canned. They add pleasing texture to stir-fries, spring rolls and noodle dishes.

White peppercorns

White peppercorns are preferred in China and Thailand, where specks of black pepper are considered unsightly. Use whole white peppercorns and grind them as required.

Wrappers

Wonton skins or wrappers are thin silky squares made from wheat flour, egg and water. They are stuffed with tasty fillings and folded into various shapes before deep-frying, steaming or serving in soup. Spring roll wrappers are larger, paper-thin and made with rice or wheat flour.

STOCK

Chinese stock is essential for authentic-tasting soups; ordinary stock or stock cubes simply do not have the right flavour. It is also invaluable when a small amount of liquid is required – it will give your dishes an extra special flavour. Stock will keep for 4–5 days in the refrigerator, or can be frozen and defrosted as required.

BASIC CHINESE STOCK

Makes about 1.5 litres/2³/₄ pints

Ingredients
900 kg/2 lb chicken pieces, such as wings, thighs and drumsticks, roughly chopped
900 kg/2 lb pork spare ribs
450 kg/1 lb ham or unsmoked gammon without rind, in one piece
4 litres/7 pints water
7 cm/2³/₄ inch thick piece fresh ginger, unpeeled and thickly sliced
1 celery stalk, roughly chopped
1 carrot, roughly chopped
3 large spring onions, green parts included, halved lengthways
2 tsp Chinese rice wine or dry sherry

1 Put the chicken, pork and ham in a large saucepan and just cover with water. Quickly bring to the boil, then drain in a colander and rinse away the scum under cold running water. Wash out the pan.

2 Return the meat to the pan and cover with the 4 litres/7 pints of water. Add the ginger, celery, carrot and spring onions, and slowly bring back to the boil, skimming off any further scum that forms. Reduce the heat to a very gentle simmer and cook, uncovered, for 2 hours.

3 Strain the stock through a colander, reserving the liquid and discarding the solids. Pour the liquid through a muslin-lined sieve. Pour back into the pan and add the rice wine. Bring to the boil, then simmer for 2–3 minutes.

4 Pour into containers, leave to cool, then store in the refrigerator. Once thoroughly chilled, remove the solidified fat from the surface.

SPICY BEEF STOCK

Makes about 1.5 litres/2³/₄ pints

Ingredients
1.5 kg/3 lb 5 oz beef brisket or boneless shin of beef, cut into large chunks
3 litres/5¹/₄ pints water
1 small onion, quartered
5 cm/2 inch thick piece fresh ginger, unpeeled and thickly sliced
5 cm/2 inch cinnamon stick
5 star anise pods
1 tsp black peppercorns
1 tsp salt

1 Put the beef in a large saucepan with enough water to cover. Quickly bring to the boil, then drain in a colander and rinse away the scum under cold running water. Wash out the pan.

2 Return the meat to the saucepan with the 3 litres/5¹/₄ pints of water, the onion, ginger, cinnamon stick, star anise, black peppercorns and salt. Slowly bring back to the boil, skimming off any further scum that forms. Reduce the heat to a very gentle simmer and cook, uncovered, for 2 hours.

3 Strain the stock through a colander, reserving the liquid and discarding the solids. Pour the liquid through a muslin-lined sieve. Pour into containers, leave to cool, then store in the refrigerator. Once thoroughly chilled, remove the solidified fat from the surface.

DIPPING SAUCES AND STANDARD SEASONINGS

Traditional dipping sauces and seasonings are served with many Chinese dishes. The spiced salt mixture is a tasty condiment for deep-fried foods.

SPRING ONION DIPPING SAUCE

Ingredients
4 tbsp finely chopped spring onions
4 tbsp finely chopped fresh ginger
2 tbsp light soy sauce
1 tsp rice vinegar
4 tbsp rapeseed oil

1 Combine the ingredients in a bowl and whisk very thoroughly until well blended. For a smooth sauce, purée in a blender.

SOY-GINGER DIPPING SAUCE

Ingredients
3 tbsp soy sauce
2 tsp very finely chopped fresh ginger

1 Combine the soy sauce and ginger in a small serving bowl. Leave to stand for 15 minutes to let the flavour develop.

SPICED SALT AND PEPPER

Ingredients
1 tbsp Szechuan pepper
1 tsp white peppercorns
5 cm/2 inch cinnamon stick, broken
2 star anise pods
5 tbsp sea salt flakes
1 tsp sugar

1 Dry-fry the Szechuan pepper, white peppercorns, cinnamon and star anise in a wok over medium heat, shaking the pan, until the Szechuan pepper begins to smoke and smell fragrant. Grind to a coarse powder with the salt, using an electric coffee grinder or a hefty mortar and pestle. Stir in the sugar then store in an airtight container for up to 2 months.

TO START

VIETNAMESE BEEF & NOODLE SOUP

Purée the shallots, garlic and ginger in a food processor or blender, pulsing several times until the purée is fairly smooth.

Heat a wok over a medium–high heat, then add the oil and stir-fry the paste for 2 minutes, taking care not to let it burn. Add the beef and stir-fry for 1 minute until brown, then pour in 1 litre/1¾ pints of the stock. Bring to a rolling boil, skimming off any scum that forms. Add the crushed peppercorns, then reduce the heat and gently simmer for 30–35 minutes, or until the meat is tender.

Meanwhile, soak the noodles in enough lukewarm water to cover for 15 minutes, or cook according to the instructions on the packet, until soft.

When the meat is tender, stir in any sticky residue that has formed at the edge of the wok. Add the remaining stock, the lime juice, fish sauce, salt and sugar. Simmer for a few minutes.

Drain the noodles and divide between individual soup bowls. Ladle the meat and broth over the top. Serve with the garnishes sprinkled over the soup.

SERVES 4

4 shallots, chopped

1 large garlic clove, chopped

2 tsp finely chopped fresh ginger

1 tbsp groundnut oil

450 g/1 lb sirloin steak, external fat removed, cut into 1-cm/½-inch cubes

1.3 litres/2¼ pints Spicy Beef Stock (see page 16)

1 tsp white peppercorns, crushed

150 g/5½ oz flat rice noodles

juice of 1 lime

2 tsp Thai fish sauce

½ tsp salt

½ tsp sugar

to garnish

4 spring onions, shredded

slivers of red chilli

3 tbsp torn coriander leaves

3 tbsp torn basil leaves

lime wedges

SPICY BEEF & MUSHROOM WONTONS

To make the filling, combine the minced steak, spring onion, mushrooms, garlic and ginger in a bowl. Mix the soy sauce, salt, pepper, five-spice seasoning and cornflour to a thin paste. Add the paste to the beef mixture, then stir in half the beaten egg (use the remainder in another recipe). Stir with a fork until very well mixed.

Separate the wonton squares and place on a tray, rotating them so one corner is facing towards you. Cover with a clean damp tea towel to prevent cracking. Working with one square at a time, place a slightly rounded teaspoon of filling in the bottom corner 1 cm/½ inch away from the point. Fold the point over the filling, then roll up two thirds of the wrapper, leaving a point at the top. Moisten the right- and left-hand corners with a dab of water. Fold one corner over the other and press lightly to seal into a bishop's mitre shape. Continue until all the wontons are filled.

Heat a large wok over a high heat. Pour in the oil and heat to 180°C/350°F or until a cube of bread browns in 30 seconds. Deep-fry the wontons in batches for 4–5 minutes until golden brown. Remove with tongs and drain on crumpled kitchen paper. Serve with the dipping sauce.

MAKES 12–15

12–15 square wonton wrappers

groundnut oil, for deep-frying

Soy-Ginger Dipping Sauce
   (see page 17), to serve

filling

125 g/4 oz lean sirloin or rump
   steak, minced

1 spring onion, green part
   included, finely chopped

2 button mushrooms, finely
   chopped

1 small garlic clove, finely chopped

½ tsp finely chopped fresh ginger

½ tsp soy sauce

¼ tsp salt

¼ tsp freshly ground white pepper

⅛ tsp Chinese five-spice
   seasoning

½ tsp cornflour

1 egg, beaten

HOT & SOUR PORK SOUP WITH BAMBOO SHOOTS

SERVES 4

2 large shiitake mushrooms

1.25 litres/2¼ pints Basic Chinese Stock (see page 16)

125 g/4½ oz pork tenderloin, thinly sliced into narrow shreds

25 g/1 oz canned sliced bamboo shoots, drained

100 g/3½ oz firm tofu, cut into 1-cm/½-inch cubes

1 tbsp Chinese rice wine or dry sherry

2 tsp light soy sauce

1 tbsp rice vinegar

¼ tsp freshly ground white pepper, or more to taste

2 spring onions, some green included, thinly sliced diagonally, to garnish

few drops sesame oil, to garnish

Remove the hard stalks from the mushrooms and slice the caps very thinly. Cut the slices in half.

Bring the stock to a rolling boil in a large wok. Reduce the heat, add the mushrooms and simmer for 5 minutes. Add the pork, bamboo shoots and tofu, and simmer for a further 5 minutes. Add the rice wine, soy sauce, vinegar and white pepper, and simmer for 1 minute.

Ladle into soup bowls and sprinkle with the spring onions and a few drops of sesame oil.

SWEET & SOUR SPARE RIBS

Combine all the marinade ingredients in a bowl. Add the pork and leave to marinate for at least 20 minutes.

Heat a large wok over a high heat. Pour in the oil and heat to 180°C/350°F or until a cube of bread browns in 30 seconds. Deep-fry the spare ribs for 8 minutes. Drain and set aside.

To prepare the sauce, mix together the vinegar, sugar, light soy sauce and ketchup. Set aside.

In a preheated wok, heat 1 tablespoon of the oil and stir-fry the pepper, onion and carrot for 2 minutes. Remove and set aside. Wipe the wok clean.

In a clean preheated wok, heat ½ tablespoon of oil and stir-fry the garlic and ginger until fragrant. Add the sauce. Bring back to the boil and add the pineapple chunks. Finally add the spare ribs and the pepper, onion and carrot. Stir until warmed through and serve immediately.

SERVES 4

450 g/1 lb spare ribs, cut into bite-sized pieces

1½ tbsp vegetable or groundnut oil, plus extra for deep-frying

1 green pepper, deseeded and roughly chopped

1 small onion, roughly chopped

1 small carrot, finely sliced

½ tsp finely chopped garlic

½ tsp finely chopped fresh ginger

100 g/3½ oz pineapple chunks

marinade

2 tsp light soy sauce

½ tsp salt

pinch of white pepper

sauce

3 tbsp white rice vinegar

2 tbsp sugar

1 tbsp light soy sauce

1 tbsp tomato ketchup

CRISPY PORK DUMPLINGS

Put the pork in a bowl and beat in the coriander, garlic, chilli, 1 tablespoon of the cornflour, the egg white and salt. Beat together to a thick, smooth texture. With damp hands shape into 16 equal portions and roll into balls.

Put a pork ball in the centre of each wonton skin. Make a paste by mixing the remaining cornflour with 1 tablespoon of water. Brush the edges of the skins with the cornflour paste and gather them up around the filling to make half into small, sack-like parcels, and the rest into triangular shapes.

Arrange the dumplings in a single layer (in batches if necessary) in the top of a steamer and cook over boiling water for 10–15 minutes, until the meat is cooked through.

Heat a large wok over a high heat. Pour in the oil and heat to 180°C/350°F or until a cube of bread browns in 30 seconds. Deep-fry for 2–3 minutes, until golden brown and crisp. Drain on kitchen paper.

Serve hot with chilli sauce.

MAKES 16

350 g/12 oz ground pork

2 tbsp finely chopped fresh coriander

1 garlic clove, crushed

1 fresh green chilli, deseeded and chopped

3 tbsp cornflour

1 egg white

½ tsp salt

16 wonton skins

1 tbsp water

vegetable or groundnut oil, for deep-frying

chilli sauce, to serve

PORK & PRAWN SPRING ROLLS

MAKES 20–25

6 dried Chinese mushrooms, soaked in warm water for 20 minutes

1 tbsp vegetable or groundnut oil, plus extra for deep-frying

225 g/8 oz pork mince

1 tsp dark soy sauce

100 g/3½ oz canned bamboo shoots, rinsed and julienned

pinch of salt

100 g/3½ oz prawns, peeled, deveined and chopped

225 g/8 oz fresh beansprouts, roughly chopped

1 tbsp finely chopped spring onions

25 spring roll wrappers

1 egg white, lightly beaten

chilli sauce, to serve

Squeeze out any excess water from the mushrooms and finely slice, discarding any tough stems.

Heat a wok over a medium–high heat, then add the oil. Stir-fry the pork until it changes colour. Add the soy sauce, bamboo shoots, mushrooms and salt. Stir over a high heat for 3 minutes.

Add the prawns and cook for 2 minutes, then add the beansprouts and cook for a further minute. Remove from the heat, stir in the spring onions and set aside to cool.

Place a tablespoon of the mixture towards the bottom of a spring roll wrapper. Roll once to secure the filling, then fold in the sides to create a 10-cm/4-inch width and continue to roll up. Seal with egg white.

Heat a large wok over a high heat. Pour in the oil and heat to 180°C/350°F or until a cube of bread browns in 30 seconds. Without overcrowding the pan, fry the rolls for about 5 minutes, until golden brown and crispy. Drain well on kitchen paper and and serve immediately with chilli sauce.

FRIED LAMB BALLS WITH SPRING ONION SAUCE

Combine the lamb, garlic and ginger in a bowl. Mix the soy sauce, wine, salt, sugar, pepper, and cornflour to a thin paste. Add the paste to the lamb mixture, then stir in the beaten egg. Stir with a fork until very well mixed. Pinch off small pieces of mixture and roll between your palms to form balls the size of a large marble.

Heat a wok over a high heat, add the oil and when it is almost smoking add the balls. Fry the balls in batches for 3 minutes, turning half-way through. Drain on crumpled kitchen paper.

Arrange a bed of shredded Chinese leaves on a serving platter. Arrange the lamb balls on top, and sprinkle with garlic chives. Divide the dipping sauce between two small bowls and serve with the lamb.

MAKES 36

450 g minced lamb

1 garlic clove, finely chopped

1 tsp finely chopped fresh ginger

1½ tbsp soy sauce

1 tsp Chinese rice wine or
   dry sherry

½ tsp salt

½ tsp sugar

½ tsp freshly ground white pepper

½ tbsp cornflour

1 egg, beaten

groundnut oil, for frying

snipped garlic chives, to garnish

shredded Chinese leaves, to serve

Spring Onion Dipping Sauce
   (see page 17), to serve

CHICKEN NOODLE SOUP

Cook the noodles in a saucepan of boiling water for 4 minutes, or according to the instructions on the packet, until soft.

Heat a wok over a medium–high heat, then add the oil. Add the chicken and stir-fry for 5 minutes, or until lightly browned. Add the white part of the spring onions, the garlic and ginger and stir-fry for 2 minutes.

Add the stock, coconut milk, curry paste, peanut butter and soy sauce. Season to taste with salt and pepper. Bring to the boil, stirring constantly, then simmer for 8 minutes, stirring occasionally. Add the pepper, peas and green spring onion tops and cook for a further 2 minutes.

Drain the noodles, then add them to the wok and heat through. Spoon into soup bowls and serve immediately.

SERVES 4–6

250 g/9 oz medium egg noodles

1 tbsp corn oil

4 skinless, boneless chicken thighs, diced

1 bunch of spring onions, sliced, white and green kept separate

2 garlic cloves, chopped

2-cm/¾-inch piece fresh ginger, finely chopped

850 ml/1½ pints chicken stock

175 ml/6 fl oz coconut milk

3 tsp Thai red curry paste

3 tbsp peanut butter

2 tbsp light soy sauce

1 small red pepper, deseeded and chopped

55 g/2 oz frozen peas

salt and pepper

ORIENTAL GLAZED CHICKEN WINGS

SERVES 4

8 chicken wings, each wing chopped into 3 pieces

5 tbsp groundnut oil

6 tbsp Basic Chinese Stock (see page 16) or water

2 tbsp chopped fresh coriander

marinade

1½ tbsp Chinese rice wine or dry sherry

1 tbsp soy sauce

1 tbsp rice vinegar

1½ tbsp sugar

¾ tsp salt

⅛ tsp Chinese five-spice seasoning

3 tbsp hoisin sauce

1 tsp finely chopped fresh ginger

To make the marinade, combine the wine, soy sauce and vinegar in a small bowl. Add the sugar, salt and five-spice seasoning, and stir until dissolved. Mix in the hoisin sauce and ginger.

Put the chopped chicken wings in a shallow dish and pour in the marinade, turning the wings to coat. Leave to marinate for 1 hour at room temperature, or overnight in the refrigerator.

Heat a wok over a high heat, add the oil and when it is almost smoking add the chicken wings and marinade. Stir-fry for 5 minutes, then sprinkle with 4 tablespoons of the stock and stir-fry for a further 4 minutes.

Using tongs, transfer the wings to a warmed serving dish, and sprinkle with the coriander. Pour off and discard most of the oil from the wok and return to the heat. Add the remaining 2 tablespoons of stock, and stir with a wooden spoon until blended, scraping up the sticky sediment. Pour into a small bowl and serve with the wings as a dipping sauce.

KARA-AGE CHICKEN

Cut the chicken into large cubes and put in a bowl. Add the shoyu, mirin, ginger and garlic and turn the chicken to coat well. Cover with clingfilm and marinate in a cool place for 20 minutes.

Heat a large wok over a high heat. Pour in the oil and heat to 180°C/350°F or until a cube of bread browns in 30 seconds.

Meanwhile, mix the potato flour with the salt in a bowl. Lift the chicken out of the marinade and shake off any excess. Drop it into the potato flour and coat well, then shake off any excess.

Add the chicken to the oil, in batches, and cook for 6 minutes, or until crisp and brown. Remove, drain on kitchen paper and keep hot while you cook the remaining chicken.

Serve with lemon wedges.

SERVES 4

6 skinless, boneless chicken thighs, about 100 g/3½ oz each

4 tbsp shoyu (Japanese soy sauce)

4 tbsp mirin

2 tsp finely grated fresh ginger

2 garlic cloves, crushed

oil, for deep-frying

70 g/2½ oz potato flour or cornflour

pinch of salt

lemon wedges, to serve

SHREDDED DUCK WITH CUCUMBER

Stack the cucumber slices, cut into thin strips and set aside. Combine the sauce ingredients in a small bowl, stirring to dissolve the sugar.

Heat a wok over a medium–high heat, then add the oils. Fry the duck breast pieces for 4–5 minutes, starting skin-side down and turning occasionally until both the skin and meat are crisp. Transfer with tongs to a cutting board and leave to cool slightly.

Lower the heat to medium. Stir-fry the shallot and ginger in the remaining oil for about 2 minutes until golden brown. Remove with a slotted spoon and drain on kitchen paper.

Remove the crisp skin from the duck pieces, and slice into shreds. Remove and discard any excess fat from the meat. Slice the meat into 5-mm/¼-inch-wide strips.

Wipe out the wok with kitchen paper and place over a medium–high heat. Add the duck meat, sauce and spring onions, and stir-fry for 2 minutes until caramelised. Season with salt and pepper, then remove from the heat.

Divide the duck mixture between the lettuce leaves, top with the cucumber strips, shallot, ginger and crushed peanuts. Roll up into parcels and serve.

SERVES 4

5-cm/2-inch piece cucumber, peeled and thinly sliced

1 tbsp groundnut oil

1 tbsp sesame oil

2 duck breasts, weighing 350 g/12 oz in total, cut into large pieces

1 large shallot, halved and sliced into crescents

2 cm/¾ inch piece fresh ginger, thinly sliced and cut into shreds

2 spring onions, shredded

4 large Webbs lettuce leaves, stalks removed

25 g/1 oz dry roasted peanuts, crushed

salt and pepper

sauce

2 tsp soy sauce

4 tsp oyster sauce

2 tsp Chinese rice wine or dry sherry

¾ tsp sugar

THAI-STYLE SEAFOOD SOUP

SERVES 4

1.25 litres/2¼ pints fish stock

1 lemon grass stem, split lengthways

pared rind of ½ lime or 1 fresh kaffir lime leaf

2.5-cm/1-inch piece fresh ginger, sliced

¼ tsp chilli paste, or to taste

4–6 spring onions

200 g/7 oz large or medium raw prawns, peeled

salt

250 g/9 oz scallops (16–20)

2 tbsp coriander leaves

fresh red chilli rings, to garnish

Place the stock in a wok with the lemon grass, lime rind, ginger and chilli paste. Bring just to the boil, then reduce the heat and simmer, covered, for 10–15 minutes.

Cut the spring onions in half lengthways, then slice crossways very thinly. Cut the prawns almost in half lengthways, keeping the tails intact. Devein if necessary.

Pour the stock through a sieve, then return to the wok and bring to a simmer, with bubbles rising at the edges and the surface trembling. Add the spring onions and cook for 2–3 minutes. Taste and season with salt, if needed. Stir in a little more chilli paste if wished.

Add the scallops and prawns and poach for 1 minute, or until they turn opaque and the prawns curl.

Drop in the coriander leaves, then ladle the soup into bowls, dividing the shellfish evenly, and garnish with chilli rings.

SPICY THAI SOUP WITH PRAWNS

Heat a wok over a high heat. Add the taramind paste, chillies, garlic, galangal, fish sauce, sugar, lime leaves and stock. Bring to the boil, stirring constantly.

Reduce the heat and add the carrots, sweet potato and baby corn cobs to the mixture in the wok.

Simmer the soup for 10 minutes or until the vegetables are just tender.

Stir the coriander, cherry tomatoes and prawns into the soup and heat through for 5 minutes.

Transfer the soup to bowls and serve hot.

SERVES 4

2 tbsp tamarind paste

4 fresh red bird's eye chillies, very finely chopped

2 garlic cloves, crushed

2.5-cm/1-inch piece fresh galangal, very finely chopped

4 tbsp Thai fish sauce

2 tbsp palm sugar or caster sugar

8 fresh kaffir lime leaves, roughly torn

1 litre/1¾ pints fish stock

115 g/4 oz very thinly sliced carrots

175 g/6 oz diced sweet potato

100 g/3½ oz baby corn cobs, halved

3 tbsp coriander, coarsely chopped

100 g/3½ oz cherry tomatoes, halved

225 g/8 oz cooked fantail prawns

SALMON & PRAWN SPRING ROLLS

Heat a non-stick wok over a high heat, add the salmon, and stir-fry for 1 minute. Remove from the wok with a slotted spoon onto a plate. Using the cooking juices from the salmon, stir-fry the vegetables with the five-spice powder until just tender, drain in a colander, then stir in the cooked salmon and prawns – the mixture should be quite dry to prevent the rolls from becoming soggy.

Divide the salmon and vegetable mixture into 8 portions. Spoon a portion along one short edge of each spring roll wrapper and roll up, tucking in the sides.

Lay the spring rolls on a non-stick baking sheet and spray lightly with vegetable oil, sprinkle with sesame seeds and bake in a preheated oven, 200°C/400°F/Gas Mark 6, for 12–15 minutes, or until golden brown. Serve the spring rolls with plum sauce.

SERVES 4

125 g/4½ oz salmon fillet, skinned, boned and cut into 3-mm/⅛-inch cubes

60 g/2¼ oz fresh beansprouts

60 g/2¼ oz Chinese cabbage, finely shredded

25 g/1 oz spring onion, finely chopped

60 g/2¼ oz red pepper, deseeded and finely sliced into strips

¼ tsp five-spice powder

60 g/2¼ oz cooked peeled prawns

4 spring roll wrappers, halved widthways

vegetable oil spray

¼ tsp sesame seeds

plum sauce, to serve

PRAWN TOASTS

MAKES 16

100 g/3½ oz raw prawns, peeled and deveined

2 egg whites, kept separate

2 tbsp cornflour

½ tsp sugar

pinch of salt

2 tbsp finely chopped coriander leaves

2 slices day-old white bread

vegetable or groundnut oil, for deep-frying

Pound the prawns to a pulp in a mortar and pestle or with the base of a cleaver.

Mix the prawns with one of the egg whites and 1 tablespoon of the cornflour. Add the sugar and salt and stir in the coriander. Mix the remaining egg white with the remaining cornflour.

Remove the crusts from the bread and cut each slice into 8 triangles. Brush the top of each piece with the egg white and cornflour mixture, then add 1 teaspoon of the prawn mixture. Smooth the top.

Heat a large wok over a high heat. Pour in the oil and heat to 180°C/350°F or until a cube of bread browns in 30 seconds. Without overcrowding the wok, cook the toasts prawn-side up for about 2 minutes. Turn and cook for a further 2 minutes, or until beginning to turn golden brown. Drain and serve warm.

CRISPY SESAME PRAWNS

Combine the flour and sesame seeds in a bowl. Stir together the curry paste, fish sauce and water in a jug until mixed. Gradually pour the liquid into the flour, stirring constantly, to make a thick batter.

Heat a large wok over a high heat. Pour in the oil and heat to 180°C/350°F or until a cube of bread browns in 30 seconds. Holding the prawns by their tails, dip them into the batter, one at a time, then carefully drop into the hot oil. Cook for 2–3 minutes, until crisp and brown. Drain on kitchen paper.

Serve immediately with chilli sauce.

TO START

SERVES 4

115 g/4 oz self-raising flour

3 tbsp sesame seeds, toasted or dry-fried

1 tsp Thai red curry paste

1 tbsp Thai fish sauce

150 ml/5 fl oz water

vegetable or groundnut oil, for deep-frying

20 large, uncooked prawns, peeled with tails intact

chilli sauce, to serve

CRISPY CRAB WONTONS

To make the filling, mix together the crabmeat, water chestnuts, chilli, spring onion, cornflour, sherry, soy sauce and lime juice in a bowl.

Spread out the wonton wrappers on a work surface and spoon an equal portion of the filling into the centre of each wonton wrapper.

Dampen the edges of the wonton wrappers with a little water and fold them in half to form triangles. Fold the 2 pointed ends in towards the centre, moisten with a little water to secure, then pinch together to seal.

Heat a large wok over a high heat. Pour in the oil and heat to 180°C/350°F or until a cube of bread browns in 30 seconds. Deep-fry the wontons in batches for 2–3 minutes, until golden brown and crisp (if you deep-fry too many at one time, the oil temperature will drop and they will be soggy).

Remove the wontons with a slotted spoon, drain on kitchen paper and serve hot, garnished with chives and lime slices.

TO START

52

MAKES 24

175 g/6 oz white crabmeat, drained if canned and thawed if frozen, flaked

50 g/1¾ oz canned water chestnuts, drained, rinsed, and chopped

1 small fresh red chilli, chopped

1 spring onion, chopped

1 tbsp cornflour

1 tsp dry sherry

1 tsp light soy sauce

½ tsp lime juice

24 wonton wrappers

vegetable oil, for deep-frying

fresh chives, to garnish

lime slices, to garnish

CHINESE VEGETABLE SOUP

SERVES 4–6

115 g/4 oz Napa cabbage

2 tbsp groundnut oil

225 g/8 oz firm marinated tofu,
   cut into 1-cm/½-inch cubes

2 garlic cloves, thinly sliced

4 spring onions, thinly sliced
   diagonally

1 carrot, thinly sliced

1 litre/1¾ pints vegetable stock

1 tbsp Chinese rice wine

2 tbsp light soy sauce

1 tsp sugar

salt and pepper

Shred the Napa cabbage and set aside. Heat a wok over a
high heat, then add the oil. Add the tofu cubes and stir-fry for
4–5 minutes until browned. Remove from the wok with a slotted
spoon and drain on kitchen paper.

   Add the garlic, spring onions and carrot to the wok and stir-fry
for 2 minutes. Pour in the stock, rice wine and soy sauce, then
add the sugar and shredded Napa cabbage. Cook over a medium
heat, stirring, for a further 1–2 minutes until heated through.

   Season with salt and pepper and return the tofu to the wok.
Ladle the soup into bowls and serve.

MUSHROOM & GINGER SOUP

Soak the dried Chinese mushrooms for at least 30 minutes in 300 ml/10 fl oz of the hot stock. Drain the mushrooms and reserve the stock. Remove the stalks of the mushrooms and discard. Slice the caps and reserve.

Cook the noodles in a saucepan of boiling water for 4 minutes, or according to the instructions on the packet, until soft. Drain well, rinse under cold water, and drain again. Set aside.

Heat a wok over a high heat, then add the oil. Add the garlic and ginger, stir and add the mushrooms. Stir over a high heat for 2 minutes.

Add the remaining stock with the reserved stock and bring to the boil. Add the mushroom ketchup and soy sauce. Stir in the beansprouts and cook until tender.

Place some noodles in each soup bowl and ladle the soup on top. Garnish with fresh coriander sprigs and serve immediately.

SERVES 4

15 g/½ oz dried Chinese mushrooms

1 litre/1¾ pints hot vegetable stock

125 g/4½ oz fine egg noodles

2 tsp sunflower oil

3 garlic cloves, crushed

2.5-cm/1-inch piece fresh ginger, finely shredded

½ tsp mushroom ketchup

1 tsp light soy sauce

125 g/4½ oz fresh beansprouts

fresh coriander sprigs, to garnish

CRISPY 'SEAWEED'

Remove and discard the tough stalks from the cabbage leaves. Wash the leaves, drain thoroughly and spread out on kitchen paper to dry.

Stack a few leaves and roll up tightly. Using a very sharp knife, slice crossways into the thinnest possible shreds. Repeat with the remaining leaves. Spread out the shreds on kitchen paper and leave until completely dry.

Heat a large wok over a high heat. Pour in the oil and heat to 180°C/350°F or until a cube of bread browns in 30 seconds. Remove the wok from the heat and add half the shredded leaves. Return the wok to the heat and deep-fry until the shreds begin to float to the surface and become crisp. Remove with a slotted spoon and drain on kitchen paper. Keep warm while you deep-fry the rest.

Tip the shreds into a warm serving bowl. Combine the sugar and salt, and sprinkle over the 'seaweed', tossing to mix.

Quickly fry the flaked almonds in the hot oil. Remove with a slotted spoon and sprinkle over the 'seaweed'. Serve warm or at room temperature.

SERVES 4

250 g/9 oz dark green cabbage leaves

groundnut oil, for deep-frying

1 tsp caster sugar

½ tsp salt

4 tbsp flaked almonds, to garnish

VEGETARIAN SPRING ROLLS

MAKES 20

6 dried Chinese mushrooms, soaked in warm water for 20 minutes

55 g/2 oz beanthread noodles, soaked in warm water for 20 minutes

2 tbsp vegetable or groundnut oil

1 tbsp finely chopped fresh ginger

100 g/3½ oz carrot, julienned

100 g/3½ oz finely shredded cabbage

1 tbsp finely sliced spring onions

1 tbsp light soy sauce

85 g/3 oz soft tofu, cut into small cubes

½ tsp salt

pinch of white pepper

pinch of sugar

20 spring roll skins

1 egg white, lightly beaten

vegetable or groundnut oil, for deep-frying

soy sauce, to serve

Squeeze out any excess water from the mushrooms and finely chop, discarding any tough stems. Drain the beanthread noodles and roughly chop.

Heat a wok over a medium–high heat, then add the oil. Toss in the ginger and cook until fragrant. Add the mushrooms and stir for about 2 minutes. Add the carrot, cabbage and spring onions and stir-fry for 1 minute. Add the beanthread noodles and light soy sauce and stir-fry for 1 minute. Add the tofu and cook for a further 1 minute. Season with the salt, pepper and sugar and mix well. Continue cooking for 1–2 minutes, or until the carrot is soft. Remove from the heat and allow to cool.

Place a level tablespoon of the filling towards the bottom of a skin. Roll once to secure the filling, then fold in the sides to create a 10-cm/4-inch width and continue to roll up. Seal with egg white.

Heat a large wok over a high heat. Pour in the oil and heat to 180°C/350°F or until a cube of bread browns in 30 seconds. Without overcrowding the pan, cook the rolls in batches for about 5 minutes, or until golden brown and crispy. Serve with a good soy sauce for dipping.

WONTONS

To make the filling, heat a wok over a high heat, then add the oil. Stir-fry the spring onions, mushrooms and beans for 1–2 minutes, until softened. Add the sweetcorn, stir well to mix, and then push the vegetables to the side. Pour in the egg. Stir until lightly set before incorporating the vegetables and adding the soy sauce, sugar and salt. Remove the wok from the heat.

Place the wonton skins in a pile on a work surface. Put a teaspoonful of the filling in the centre of the top skin. Brush the edges with beaten egg and fold in half diagonally to make a small triangular package. Repeat with the remaining skins and filling.

Heat a large wok over a high heat. Pour in the oil and heat to 180°C/350°F or until a cube of bread browns in 30 seconds. Add the packages, in batches, and deep-fry for 3–4 minutes, until they are golden brown. Remove them from the wok with a slotted spoon and drain on kitchen paper. Keep them warm while you cook the remaining wontons. Serve hot with plum or chilli sauce.

SERVES 4

2 tbsp vegetable or groundnut oil

6 spring onions, chopped

125 g/4½ oz mushrooms, chopped

55 g/2 oz French beans, chopped

55 g/2 oz sweetcorn kernels, drained if canned

1 egg, beaten

3 tbsp Thai soy sauce

1 tbsp jaggery or soft light brown sugar

½ tsp salt

24 wonton skins

1 egg, beaten

vegetable or groundnut oil, for deep-frying

plum or chilli sauce, to serve

PICKLED BABY CUCUMBERS

Heat a wok over a medium–high heat, then add the oil. Cook the cucumber for 3–5 minutes, until they are bright green. Drain and set aside. When cool, score the skin many times on all sides. Place in a large dish.

Combine the vinegar, salt, sugar and chillies and pour over the cucumbers, immersing them in the liquid. Marinate for 24 hours, then serve cold in chunks.

SERVES 4

1 tbsp vegetable or groundnut oil, for frying

400 g/14 oz baby cucumbers

500 ml/18 fl oz white rice vinegar

1 tbsp salt

3 tbsp sugar

3 red bird's eye chillies, deseeded and finely chopped

VEGETABLES & SALADS

CLASSIC STIR-FRIED VEGETABLES

Heat a wok over a high heat, then add the oil. Stir-fry three quarters of the chopped spring onions with the garlic and ginger for 30 seconds.

Add the broccoli, pepper and red cabbage and stir-fry for 1–2 minutes. Mix in the baby corn and mushrooms and stir-fry for a further 1–2 minutes.

Finally, add the beansprouts and water chestnuts and cook for 2 minutes. Pour in the soy sauce and stir well.

Serve immediately, garnished with the remaining spring onions.

SERVES 4

3 tbsp sesame oil

8 spring onions, chopped

1 garlic clove, crushed

1 tbsp grated fresh ginger

1 head of broccoli, cut into florets

1 orange or yellow pepper, deseeded and roughly chopped

125 g/4½ oz red cabbage, shredded

125 g/4½ oz baby corn

175 g/6 oz portobello mushrooms, thinly sliced

200 g/7 oz fresh beansprouts

250 g/9 oz canned water chestnuts, drained

4 tsp light soy sauce, or to taste

SWEET-&-SOUR VEGETABLES WITH CASHEW NUTS

Heat a wok over a high heat, then add both the oils. Add the onions and stir-fry for 1–2 minutes until beginning to soften.

Add the carrots, courgettes and broccoli and stir-fry for 2–3 minutes. Add the mushrooms, bok choi, sugar, soy sauce and vinegar and stir-fry for 1–2 minutes.

Meanwhile, heat a dry, heavy-based frying pan over a high heat, add the cashew nuts and cook, shaking the frying pan frequently, until lightly toasted. Sprinkle the cashew nuts over the stir fry and serve immediately.

SERVES 4

1 tbsp vegetable or groundnut oil

1 tsp chilli oil

2 onions, sliced

2 carrots, thinly sliced

2 courgettes, thinly sliced

115 g/4 oz head of broccoli, cut into florets

115 g/4 oz white mushrooms, sliced

115 g/4 oz small bok choi, halved

2 tbsp brown sugar

2 tbsp Thai soy sauce

1 tbsp rice vinegar

55 g/2 oz cashew nuts

MIXED VEGETABLES WITH BASIL

SERVES 4

2 tbsp vegetable or groundnut oil, plus extra for shallow frying

2 garlic cloves, chopped

1 onion, sliced

115 g/4 oz baby corn, cut in half diagonally

½ cucumber, peeled, halved, deseeded and sliced

225 g/8 oz canned water chestnuts, drained and rinsed

55 g/2 oz mangetout

115 g/4 oz shiitake mushrooms, halved

1 red pepper, deseeded and thinly sliced

1 tbsp soft light brown sugar

2 tbsp Thai soy sauce

1 tbsp Thai fish sauce

1 tbsp rice vinegar

8–12 sprigs fresh Thai basil

freshly cooked plain rice, to serve

Heat a wok over a high heat, then add the oil. Stir-fry the garlic and onion for 1–2 minutes. Add the baby corn, cucumber, water chestnuts, mangetout, mushrooms and red pepper and stir-fry for 2–3 minutes, until starting to soften.

Add the sugar, soy sauce, fish sauce and vinegar and gradually bring to the boil. Simmer for 1–2 minutes.

Meanwhile, heat enough oil for shallow frying in a wok and, when hot, add the basil sprigs. Cook for 20–30 seconds, until crisp. Remove with a slotted spoon and drain on kitchen paper.

Garnish the vegetable stir fry with the crispy basil and serve immediately with rice.

BAMBOO SHOOTS WITH TOFU

Squeeze out any excess water from the mushrooms and finely slice, discarding any tough stems. Blanch the bok choi in a large saucepan of boiling water for 30 seconds. Drain and set aside.

Heat a large wok over a high heat. Pour in the oil and heat to 180°C/350°F or until a cube of bread browns in 30 seconds. Cook the tofu cubes until golden brown. Remove, then drain and set aside.

Heat a wok over a high heat, then add 1 tablespoon of the oil. Toss in the mushrooms and bok choi and stir. Add the tofu and bamboo shoots with the oyster and soy sauces. Heat through and serve.

SERVES 4–6

3 dried Chinese mushrooms, soaked in warm water for 20 minutes

55 g/2 oz baby bok choi

vegetable or groundnut oil, for deep-frying

450 g/1 lb firm tofu, cut into 2.5-cm/1-inch squares

55 g/2 oz fresh or canned bamboo shoots, rinsed and finely sliced (if using fresh shoots, boil in water first for 30 minutes)

1 tsp oyster sauce

1 tsp light soy sauce

STIR-FRIED BEANSPROUTS

Heat a wok over a medium–high heat, then add the oil. Stir-fry the beansprouts with the spring onion for about 1 minute. Add the salt and sugar and stir.

Remove from the heat and serve immediately.

SERVES 4

1 tbsp vegetable or groundnut oil

225 g/8 oz fresh beansprouts

2 tbsp finely chopped spring onion

½ tsp salt

pinch of sugar

SPICY FRENCH BEANS

SERVES 4

200 g/7 oz French beans, trimmed
and cut diagonally into
3–4 pieces

2 tbsp vegetable or groundnut oil

4 dried chillies, cut into 2–3 pieces

½ tsp Szechuan peppers

1 garlic clove, finely sliced

6 thin slices fresh ginger

2 spring onions, white part only,
cut diagonally into thin pieces

pinch of sea salt

Blanch the beans in a large pan of boiling water for 30 seconds.
Drain and set aside.

Heat a wok over a medium–high heat, then add 1 tablespoon
of the oil. Stir-fry the beans for about 5 minutes, or until they are
beginning to wrinkle. Remove from the wok and set aside.

Add the remaining oil to the wok and stir-fry the chillies and
peppers until they are fragrant. Add the garlic, ginger and spring
onions and stir-fry until they begin to soften. Add the beans and
toss to mix, then add the sea salt and serve immediately.

STIR-FRIED BROCCOLI

Heat a wok over a medium–high heat, then add the oil. Stir-fry the broccoli for 4–5 minutes.

In a small bowl, combine the soy sauce, cornflour, sugar, ginger, garlic and chilli flakes. Add the mixture to the broccoli. Cook over a low heat, stirring constantly, for 2–3 minutes, until the sauce thickens slightly.

Transfer to a serving dish, garnish with the sesame seeds and serve immediately.

SERVES 4

2 tbsp vegetable oil

2 medium heads of broccoli, cut into florets

2 tbsp light soy sauce

1 tsp cornflour

1 tbsp caster sugar

1 tsp grated fresh ginger

1 garlic clove, crushed

pinch of hot chilli flakes

1 tsp toasted sesame seeds, to garnish

CAULIFLOWER & BEANS WITH CASHEW NUTS

Heat a wok over a medium–high heat, then add both the oils. Stir-fry the onion and garlic until softened. Add the curry paste and stir-fry for 1–2 minutes.

Add the cauliflower and beans and stir-fry for 3–4 minutes, until softened. Pour in the stock and soy sauce and simmer for 1–2 minutes. Serve immediately, garnished with the cashew nuts.

SERVES 4

1 tbsp vegetable or groundnut oil

1 tbsp chilli oil

1 onion, chopped

2 garlic cloves, chopped

2 tbsp Thai red curry paste

1 small cauliflower, cut into florets

175 g/6 oz French beans, cut into 7.5-cm/3-inch lengths

150 ml/5 fl oz vegetable stock

2 tbsp Thai soy sauce

50 g/1¾ oz toasted cashew nuts, to garnish

CHUNKY POTATOES WITH CORIANDER LEAVES

SERVES 6–8

4 potatoes, peeled and cut into
  large chunks

vegetable or groundnut oil,
  for frying

100 g/3½ oz pork, not too lean,
  finely chopped or minced

1 green pepper, deseeded and
  finely chopped

1 tbsp finely chopped spring
  onions, white part only

2 tsp salt

½ tsp white pepper

pinch of sugar

2–3 tbsp cooking water from the
  potatoes

2 tbsp chopped coriander leaves

Boil the potatoes in a large saucepan of boiling water for
15–25 minutes, or until cooked. Drain, reserving some of
the water.

Heat a wok over a medium–high heat, then add plenty of the
oil. Cook the potatoes until golden. Drain and set aside.

Heat a clean wok over a medium–high heat, add 1 tablespoon
of the oil and stir-fry the pork, pepper and spring onions for
1 minute. Season with the salt, pepper and sugar and stir-fry
for a further 1 minute.

Stir in the potato chunks and add the water. Cook for
2–3 minutes, or until the potatoes are warmed through. Turn
off the heat, then stir in the coriander and serve warm.

SZECHUAN FRIED AUBERGINE

Heat a wok over a medium–high heat, then add 2 tablespoons of
the oil. Cook the aubergine pieces for 3–4 minutes, or until lightly
browned. Drain on kitchen paper and set aside.

Heat a clean wok over a medium–high heat, then add
2 tablespoons of the oil. Add the chilli bean sauce and stir-fry
rapidly, then add the ginger and garlic and stir until fragrant.
Add the stock, sugar and light soy sauce. Toss in the fried
aubergine pieces and simmer for 2 minutes. Stir in the spring
onions and serve.

SERVES 4

vegetable or groundnut oil,
   for frying

4 aubergines, halved lengthways
   and cut diagonally into 5-cm/
   2-inch pieces

1 tbsp chilli bean sauce

2 tsp finely chopped fresh ginger

2 tsp finely chopped garlic

2–3 tbsp chicken stock

1 tsp sugar

1 tsp light soy sauce

3 spring onions, finely chopped

STIR-FRIED BUTTERNUT SQUASH

Cut the squash in two between the neck and the rounded part. Remove the skin from each piece. Quarter the rounded part and remove the seeds and fibres. Slice lengthways into thin segments. Slice the neck in half lengthways, then crossways into thin semicircles.

Remove and discard the tough stalks from the mushrooms, and thinly slice the caps.

Heat a wok over a medium–high heat, then add the oil. Add half the crushed peppercorns and coriander seeds. Stir for a few seconds, then add the squash in small batches. Fry for 5–7 minutes, carefully turning with tongs, until lightly browned and just tender. Sprinkle with sea salt flakes. Using a slotted spoon, transfer to a large sieve set over a bowl.

Add the mushrooms to the wok and fry for 4–5 minutes, using some of the oil drained from the squash. Add the garlic and lemon zest, and fry for another minute. Sprinkle with sea salt flakes and the rest of the coriander seeds and peppercorns. Add to the squash.

Pour any oil drained from the vegetables into the wok. Stir in the vinegar and stock, and simmer for a few seconds until slightly reduced.

Arrange the spinach on individual serving plates. Pile the vegetables on top, then pour over the juices from the wok. Sprinkle with coriander and serve at once.

SERVES 2

1 butternut squash, weighing about 500 g/18 oz

6 large shiitake mushrooms

5 tbsp rapeseed oil

½ tsp white peppercorns, crushed

½ tsp coriander seeds, crushed

2 large garlic cloves, thinly sliced

finely grated zest of ½ lemon

½ tbsp rice vinegar

4 tbsp chicken or vegetable stock

2 good handfuls of baby spinach, stalks removed

sea salt flakes

chopped fresh coriander, to garnish

STIR-FRIED TOFU WITH BEANSPROUTS

SERVES 2–3

1½ tbsp light soy sauce

1 tbsp oyster sauce

2 tbsp chicken stock or Basic
   Chinese Stock (see page 16)

groundnut oil, for deep-frying

350 g/12 oz firm tofu, cubed

2 large garlic cloves, thinly sliced

115 g/4 oz mangetout, trimmed
   and halved diagonally

4 spring onions, sliced diagonally
   into 2.5-cm/1-inch pieces

115 g/4 oz beansprouts

salt and pepper

½ bunch of garlic chives or
   ordinary chives, snipped into
   2.5-cm/1-inch lengths,
   to garnish

few drops sesame oil, to garnish

Combine the soy sauce, oyster sauce and chicken stock in a small
bowl and set aside.

Heat a wok over a high heat, then add the oil. Heat the oil to
180°C/350°F or until a cube of bread browns in 30 seconds, then
add the tofu and fry for 5–7 minutes until golden brown, turning
with tongs. Remove with a slotted spoon and drain on kitchen
paper. Season with salt and freshly ground black pepper.

Pour the oil from the wok, reserving 1 tablespoon (use the rest
in another dish), and wipe out the wok. Heat the reserved oil,
add the garlic and stir-fry for a few seconds to flavour the oil. Add
the mangetout and spring onions, and stir-fry for 2 minutes.

Add the beansprouts and soy sauce mixture. Stir-fry for
1 minute, then toss in the fried tofu and stir to mix. Sprinkle
with the chives and a few drops of sesame oil, and serve at once.

SZECHUAN NUMBING BEEF SALAD

Slice the beef into neat strips measuring about 1 x 4 cm/
½ x 1½ inches. Combine the marinade ingredients and pour over
the beef. Leave at room temperature for 30 minutes or in the
refrigerator for up to 2 days.

Cook the noodles in a saucepan of boiling water for 4 minutes,
or according to the instructions on the packet, until soft. Allow
to cool. Snip into shorter lengths. Whisk the dressing ingredients
until well blended. Combine the noodles, onion, radishes and
salad leaves in a large bowl. Whisk the dressing again and pour
two thirds of it over the salad. Toss to distribute the noodles,
then divide between individual serving plates.

Heat a wok over a medium–high heat, then add the groundnut
oil and the Szechuan pepper. Stir for a few seconds to flavour the
oil. Add the beef and marinade, and stir-fry for 4–5 minutes until
caramelised. Remove with a slotted spoon, and scatter over the
salad. Pour over the remaining dressing.

SERVES 4

350 g/12 oz sirloin steak, external
   fat removed

90 g/3½ oz egg noodles

1 small red onion, halved and
   thinly sliced into crescents

6 radishes, sliced

4 good handfuls of peppery leaves
   such as tatsoi, mustard greens
   and rocket

1½ tbsp groundnut oil

1 tsp Szechuan pepper, crushed

marinade

4 tsp Chinese rice wine or dry
   sherry

½ tbsp soy sauce

4 tsp sugar

2 tbsp hoisin sauce

2.5-cm/1-inch piece fresh ginger,
   squeezed in a garlic press

dressing

2 tsp Szechuan pepper, crushed

1½ tbsp light soy sauce

1½ tbsp rice vinegar

2 tbsp cold-pressed sesame oil

PORK & CUCUMBER SALAD

Trim the tenderloin of any sinew and fat, and thinly slice diagonally. Cut each slice in half lengthways. Put in a bowl with the spring onions.

Peel the cucumber, halve lengthways and scoop out the seeds. Thinly slice diagonally and put in a bowl.

Next make the marinade. Using a large mortar and pestle, pound the chopped chillies and the sugar to a watery red paste. Add the fish sauce, lime juice and rice vinegar, stirring to dissolve the sugar. Pour into a measuring jug. Pour one half over the pork and onions, and one half over the cucumber. Leave to marinate for 1 hour, then drain, reserving the marinade.

Put the shredded lettuce, coriander and mint in a bowl, and toss to mix. Divide between individual serving plates. Arrange the cucumber slices on top and dress with the reserved marinade.

Mix the nuts with the lime zest, salt and sugar.

Drain the pork and discard the marinade. Heat a wok over a high heat, then add the oils. Stir-fry the pork for 5 minutes until cooked through and slightly caramelised. Arrange the pork slices on top of the cucumber and sprinkle with the nut mixture. Serve at once.

SERVES 4

450 g/1 lb pork tenderloin

6 spring onions, halved lengthways and sliced into 3

1 ridge cucumber

4 handfuls shredded crisp lettuce

20 g/¾ oz coriander leaves

10 g/¼ oz mint leaves

4 tbsp dry-roasted peanuts, lightly crushed

finely grated zest of 1 lime

1 tsp salt

1 tsp sugar

2 tsp sesame oil

1 tbsp groundnut oil

marinade

2 small red chillies, deseeded and very finely chopped

4 tbsp sugar

3 tbsp Thai fish sauce

4 tbsp lime juice

4 tbsp rice vinegar

CHINESE
CHICKEN SALAD

SERVES 4

3 boneless, skinless chicken
   breasts, weighing 450 g/1 lb in
   total, cut into bite-sized pieces

2 tsp soy sauce

¼ tsp freshly ground white pepper

2 tbsp groundnut oil, plus extra
   for deep-frying

50 g/1¾ oz thin rice noodles

½ head Chinese leaves, thinly
   sliced diagonally

3 spring onions, green parts
   included, sliced diagonally

40 g/1 ½ oz almonds with skin,
   sliced lengthways

2 tsp sesame seeds, to garnish

dressing

5 tbsp olive oil

3 tbsp rice vinegar

3 tbsp light soy sauce

a few drops sesame oil

salt and pepper

Sprinkle the chicken with the soy sauce and white pepper.
Combine the dressing ingredients and whisk to blend.

   Heat a wok over a high heat, then add the groundnut oil.
Stir-fry the chicken for 4–5 minutes until brown and crisp. Drain
on kitchen paper and allow to cool. Wipe out the wok.

   Pour enough groundnut oil for deep-frying into the wok. Heat
to 180°C/350°F or until a cube of bread browns in 30 seconds,
then fry a few noodles at a time until puffed up and crisp. Drain
on kitchen paper.

   Arrange the Chinese leaves in a shallow serving dish. Place the
noodles in a pile on top of the leaves on one side of the dish.
Arrange the chicken, spring onion and almonds in the remaining
space. Whisk the dressing again and pour over the salad. Dress
with the sesame seeds and serve.

GINGERED
CHICKEN SALAD

Cut the chicken into large cubes, each about 2.5 cm/1 inch. Mix together the spring onions, ginger, crushed garlic and 2 tablespoons of the oil in a shallow dish and add the chicken. Cover and marinate for at least 3 hours. Lift the meat out of the marinade and set aside.

Heat a wok over a high heat, then add the remaining oil. Cook the onion for 1–2 minutes. Add the garlic, baby corn, mangetout and pepper and cook for 2–3 minutes, until just tender. Add the cucumber, half the soy sauce, the sugar and the basil and mix gently.

Soak the noodles for 2–3 minutes or until tender, and drain well. Sprinkle the remaining soy sauce over them and arrange on plates. Top with the cooked vegetables.

Add a little more oil to the wok if necessary and cook the chicken over a fairly high heat until browned on all sides and cooked through. Arrange the chicken cubes on top of the salad and serve hot or warm.

SERVES 4

4 skinless, boneless chicken breasts

4 spring onions, chopped

2.5-cm/1-inch piece fresh ginger, chopped finely

4 garlic cloves, 2 crushed and 2 chopped

3 tbsp vegetable or groundnut oil

1 onion, sliced

2 garlic cloves, chopped

115 g/4 oz baby corn, halved

115 g/4 oz mangetout, halved lengthways

1 red pepper, deseeded and sliced

7.5-cm/3-inch piece cucumber, peeled, deseeded and sliced

4 tbsp Thai soy sauce

1 tbsp soft light brown sugar

few Thai basil leaves

175 g/6 oz fine egg noodles

RICE & TURKEY SALAD

Set aside 3 tablespoons of the chicken stock and bring the remainder to the boil in a large saucepan. Add the rice and cook for 30 minutes or until tender. Drain and cool slightly.

Heat a wok over a high heat, then add 1 tablespoon of the oil. Stir-fry the turkey over medium heat for 3–4 minutes or until cooked through. Using a slotted spoon, transfer the turkey to a dish. Add the mangetout and mushrooms to the wok and stir-fry for 1 minute. Add the reserved stock, bring to the boil, then reduce the heat, cover and simmer for 3–4 minutes. Transfer the vegetables to the dish and cool slightly.

Thoroughly mix together the rice, turkey, mangetout, mushrooms, nuts, coriander and garlic chives, then season to taste with salt and pepper. Drizzle with the remaining corn oil and the vinegar and garnish with fresh garlic chives. Serve warm.

SERVES 4

1 litre/1¾ pints chicken stock

200 g/7 oz mixed long-grain and wild rice

2 tbsp corn oil

225 g/8 oz skinless, boneless turkey breast, trimmed of all visible fat and cut into thin strips

115 g/4 oz mangetout

115 g/4 oz oyster mushrooms, torn into pieces

25 g/1 oz shelled pistachio nuts, finely chopped

2 tbsp chopped fresh coriander

1 tbsp snipped fresh garlic chives

salt and pepper

1 tbsp balsamic vinegar

fresh garlic chives, to garnish

DUCK SALAD

SERVES 4

4 boneless duck breasts, skin on

1 lemon grass stem, broken into three and each cut in half lengthways

3 tbsp vegetable or groundnut oil

2 tbsp sesame oil

1 tsp Thai fish sauce

1 fresh green chilli, deseeded and chopped

2 tbsp Thai red curry paste

½ fresh pineapple, peeled and sliced

7.5-cm/3-inch piece cucumber, peeled, deseeded and sliced

3 tomatoes, cut into wedges

1 onion, sliced thinly

dressing

juice of 1 lemon

2 garlic cloves, crushed

1 tsp jaggery

2 tbsp vegetable or groundnut oil

Unwrap the duck and let the skin dry out overnight in the refrigerator.

The following day, slash the skin side 5–6 times. Mix together the lemon grass, 2 tablespoons of the vegetable oil, all the sesame oil, fish sauce, chilli and curry paste in a shallow dish and place the duck breasts in the mixture. Turn to coat and to rub the marinade into the meat. Chill for 2–3 hours.

Heat a wok over a medium–high heat, then add the remaining oil. Cook the duck skin-side down, over a medium heat, for 3–4 minutes until the skin is browned and crisp and the meat is cooked most of the way through.

Turn the breasts over and cook until browned and the meat is cooked to your liking.

Meanwhile, arrange the pineapple, cucumber, tomatoes, and onion on a platter. Mix together the dressing ingredients and pour over the top.

Lift the duck out of the wok and slice thickly. Arrange the duck slices on top of the salad and serve while still hot.

CHINESE
PRAWN SALAD

Cook the noodles in a saucepan of boiling water for 4 minutes, or according to the instructions on the packet, until soft. Drain thoroughly and pat dry with kitchen paper.

Heat a wok over a high heat, then add the sunflower oil. Add the noodles and stir-fry for 5 minutes, tossing frequently.

Remove the wok from the heat and add the sesame oil, sesame seeds and beansprouts, tossing to mix well.

Mix together the mango, spring onions, radishes, prawns, soy sauce and sherry in a separate bowl. Toss the prawn mixture with the noodles. Alternatively, arrange the noodles around the edge of a serving plate and pile the prawn mixture into the centre. Serve immediately.

SERVES 4

250 g/9 oz thin egg noodles

3 tbsp sunflower oil

1 tbsp sesame oil

1 tbsp sesame seeds

175 g/6 oz fresh beansprouts

1 mango, peeled, pitted and sliced

6 spring onions, sliced

75 g/2¾ oz radishes, sliced

350 g/12 oz cooked peeled prawns

2 tbsp light soy sauce

1 tbsp sherry

CARAMELISED TUNA SALAD

To make the dressing, heat a small wok over high heat. Add the oil and fry the ginger and chilli for a few seconds. Add the soy sauce, fish sauce and tamarind paste. Stir for 30 seconds, then add the sugar and stir until dissolved. Remove the wok from the heat and set aside.

Rinse the beansprouts in boiling water and drain. Blot dry with kitchen paper. Peel the cucumber, halve lengthways and scoop out the seeds. Thinly slice the flesh diagonally.

Put the beansprouts, cucumber, coriander and mint leaves in a bowl. Season with a pinch of salt and a few drops of toasted sesame oil. Toss to combine, then divide between individual serving plates.

Heat a wok over a high heat, then add the groundnut and sesame oils. Quickly stir-fry the tuna, turning with tongs, until coloured on the outside but still slightly red in the middle. Arrange the tuna chunks on top of the salad.

Reheat the dressing, thinning with a spoonful of water if necessary, and pour over the tuna. Sprinkle with the crushed peanuts and serve at once.

SERVES 4

175 g/6 oz fresh beansprouts

10 cm/4 inch piece of cucumber

20 g/³⁄₄ oz coriander leaves

20 g/³⁄₄ oz mint leaves

1 tsp sesame oil, plus a few drops for drizzling

1 tbsp groundnut oil

450 g/1 lb fresh tuna, cut into 2.5-cm/1-inch chunks

salt

2 tbsp salted roasted peanuts, crushed, to garnish

dressing

2 tsp rapeseed oil

1 tsp finely chopped fresh ginger

¹⁄₂–1 small red chilli, deseeded and finely chopped

4 tbsp light soy sauce

1 tbsp Thai fish sauce

1 tbsp tamarind paste

6 tbsp soft brown sugar

RAINBOW
SALAD

SERVES 3–4

6 large shiitake mushrooms

10 spring onions, green part
  included

6 carrots

3 tbsp rapeseed oil

1 red pepper, deseeded and finely
  sliced

8 baby corn, halved diagonally

250 g fresh beansprouts

salt

a few small mint leaves, to garnish

4 tbsp toasted coconut ribbons,
  to garnish

dressing

½–1 green chilli, deseeded and
  very finely chopped

1 tsp sugar

1½ tbsp lime juice

2 tsp fish sauce

2 tbsp chopped mint

2 tbsp rapeseed oil

6 tbsp coconut cream

salt

First make the dressing. Using a mortar and pestle, pound the chopped chilli and the sugar to a watery green paste. Add the lime juice, fish sauce and a pinch of salt, stirring to dissolve the sugar. Pour into a blender with the mint, oil and coconut cream. Purée until smooth and set aside.

Remove and discard the tough stalks from the mushrooms, and thinly slice the caps. Halve, core and deseed the pepper, and slice into very thin slivers. Halve the spring onions lengthways, then slice into 2.5-cm/1-inch lengths, keeping the green and white parts separate.

Using a swivel peeler, shave the carrots into thin slivers.

Heat a wok over a high heat, then add 3 tablespoons of the oil. Stir-fry the mushrooms, red pepper, baby corn and the white spring onions for 2 minutes. Add the carrots, beansprouts, green spring onions and salt to taste. Toss for 1 minute until the vegetables are only just cooked and still crunchy.

Transfer to a colander set over a bowl to cool. Discard any drained liquid and tip into a serving bowl. Toss with the dressing, then sprinkle with mint leaves and the toasted coconut ribbons. Serve at room temperature.

AUBERGINE & ONION SALAD

Heat a wok over a high heat, then add half the oil. Cook the onion, shallot and spring onions together for 1–2 minutes, until just softened but not browned. Lift out and set aside.

Add the aubergine cubes, in batches if necessary, adding more oil as needed, and cook until they are crisp and golden brown.

Return the onions to the wok and add the curry paste, soy sauce and sugar. Add the creamed coconut and water and cook until dissolved. Stir in most of the coriander, the basil and the parsley.

Toss the rocket in the sweet chilli sauce and serve with the aubergine and onion salad. Garnish with the remaining herbs.

SERVES 4

4 tbsp vegetable or groundnut oil

1 onion, sliced

4 shallots, chopped finely

4 spring onions, sliced

350 g/12 oz aubergines, cubed

2 tbsp Thai green curry paste

2 tbsp Thai soy sauce

1 tsp soft light brown sugar

115 g/4 oz block creamed coconut, chopped

3 tbsp water

small handful of fresh coriander, chopped

few Thai basil leaves, chopped

small handful of fresh parsley, chopped

115 g/4 oz rocket leaves

2 tbsp sweet chilli sauce

HOT-&-SOUR VEGETABLE SALAD

Heat a wok over a medium–high heat and add the oils. Sauté the onion and ginger for 1–2 minutes until they start to soften. Add the vegetables and stir-fry for 2–3 minutes until they have softened slightly. Remove from the heat and set aside.

Mix together the dressing ingredients. Transfer the vegetables to a serving plate and drizzle the dressing over. Serve warm immediately, or let the flavours develop and serve cold.

SERVES 4

2 tbsp vegetable or groundnut oil

1 tbsp chilli oil

1 onion, sliced

2.5-cm/1-inch piece fresh ginger, grated

1 small head of broccoli, cut into florets

2 carrots, cut into short thin sticks

1 red pepper, deseeded and cut into squares

1 yellow pepper, deseeded and cut into strips

55 g/2 oz mangetout, trimmed and halved

55 g/2 oz baby corn, halved

dressing

2 tbsp vegetable or groundnut oil

1 tsp chilli oil

1 tbsp rice wine vinegar

juice of 1 lime

½ tsp Thai fish sauce

MEAT

BEEF CHOW MEIN

Combine all the marinade ingredients in a bowl and marinate the beef for at least 20 minutes.

Cook the noodles in a saucepan of boiling water for 4 minutes, or according to the instructions on the packet, until soft. Drain, then rinse under cold running water and set aside.

Heat a wok over a medium–high heat, then add the oil. Stir-fry the beef for about 1 minute, until the meat has changed colour, then add the onion and cook for 1 minute, then add the green pepper and beansprouts. Cook until any water from the vegetables has evaporated.

Add the salt, sugar, rice wine and soy sauces. Stir in the noodles and toss for 1 minute. Finally, stir in the spring onion and serve.

SERVES 4

280 g/10 oz fillet steak, cut into thin strips

225 g/8 oz medium egg noodles

2 tbsp vegetable or groundnut oil

1 onion, finely sliced

1 green pepper, deseeded and finely sliced

140 g/5 oz fresh beansprouts

1 tsp salt

pinch of sugar

2 tsp Chinese rice wine

2 tbsp light soy sauce

1 tbsp dark soy sauce

1 tbsp finely shredded spring onion

marinade

1 tsp light soy sauce

dash of sesame oil

$\frac{1}{2}$ tsp Chinese rice wine

pinch of white pepper

STIR-FRIED BEEF WITH BEANSPROUTS

Slice the spring onions lengthways into thin strips, reserving some for garnish.

Heat a wok over a medium–high heat, then add the oil. Add the spring onions, garlic and ginger and stir-fry for 2–3 minutes, until softened. Add the beef and continue stir-frying for 4–5 minutes, or until evenly browned.

Add the red pepper and stir-fry for a further 3–4 minutes. Add the chilli and beansprouts and stir-fry for 2 minutes. Mix together the lemon grass, peanut butter, coconut milk, vinegar, soy sauce and sugar in a bowl, then stir into the wok.

Meanwhile, cook the noodles in a saucepan of boiling water for 4 minutes, or according to the packet directions, until soft. Drain and stir into the pan, tossing to mix evenly. Season to taste with salt and pepper. Sprinkle with the reserved spring onions and serve hot.

SERVES 4

1 bunch of spring onions

2 tbsp corn oil

1 garlic clove, crushed

1 tsp finely chopped fresh ginger

500 g/1 lb 2 oz lean beef fillet, cut into thin strips

1 large red pepper, deseeded and sliced

1 small fresh red chilli, deseeded and chopped

225 g/8 oz fresh beansprouts

1 small lemon grass stem, finely chopped

2 tbsp smooth peanut butter

4 tbsp coconut milk

1 tbsp rice vinegar or white wine vinegar

1 tbsp soy sauce

1 tsp light brown sugar

250 g/9 oz medium egg noodles

salt and pepper

HOT SESAME
BEEF

SERVES 4

500 g/1 lb 2 oz beef fillet, cut into thin strips

1½ tbsp sesame seeds

125 ml/4 fl oz beef stock

2 tbsp light soy sauce

2 tbsp grated fresh ginger

2 garlic cloves, finely chopped

1 tsp cornflour

½ tsp chilli flakes

3 tbsp sesame oil

1 large head of broccoli, cut into florets

1 orange pepper, deseeded and thinly sliced

1 fresh red chilli, deseeded and finely sliced

1 tbsp chilli oil, or to taste

1 tbsp chopped fresh coriander, to garnish

Mix the beef with 1 tablespoon of the sesame seeds in a small bowl. In a separate bowl, whisk together the stock, soy sauce, ginger, garlic, cornflour and chilli flakes.

Heat a wok over a medium–high heat, then add 2 tablespoons of the sesame oil. Stir-fry the beef for 2–3 minutes. Remove and set aside.

Discard any oil left in the wok, then wipe with kitchen paper to remove any stray sesame seeds. Heat the remaining oil in the wok, add the broccoli, orange pepper, chilli and chilli oil, and stir-fry for 2–3 minutes. Stir in the stock mixture, cover and simmer for 2 minutes.

Return the beef to the wok and simmer until the juices thicken, stirring occasionally. Cook for a futher 1–2 minutes.

Sprinkle with the remaining sesame seeds. Serve garnished with chopped coriander.

DAN DAN
NOODLES

Heat a wok over a medium–high heat, then add the oil. Toss in the chilli and peppers, then add the meat and stir rapidly. When the meat has changed colour, add the light soy sauce and continue to cook until the meat is well browned.

Carefully mix together the sauce ingredients and pour into 4 serving dishes.

Soak the noodles in enough lukewarm water to cover for 15 minutes, or cook according to the instructions on the packet, until soft. Drain and divide among the dishes.

Top with the meat mixture, then sprinkle with the roasted peanuts and serve at once. Mix well before eating.

SERVES 4

1 tbsp vegetable or groundnut oil

1 large dried chilli, deseeded and snipped into 3 pieces

½ tsp Szechuan peppers

100 g/3½ oz fresh beef mince

2 tsp light soy sauce

300 g/10½ oz fine rice noodles

1 tbsp roasted peanuts, chopped

sauce

1 tbsp preserved vegetables

½ tsp Szechuan peppers, lightly roasted and crushed

100 ml/3½ fl oz chicken stock

1 tsp black rice vinegar

1 tsp chilli oil

1 tsp dark soy sauce

1 tbsp light soy sauce

1 tbsp sesame paste

a few drops of sesame oil

2 spring onions, finely chopped

BEEF NOODLES WITH OYSTER SAUCE

To make the marinade, stir together the ingredients in a non-metallic bowl. Stir in the beef so all the slices are coated, then set aside to marinate for at least 15 minutes.

Meanwhile, cook the noodles in a saucepan of boiling water for 4 minutes, or according to the packet instructions, until soft. Drain, rinse and drain again, then set aside.

Heat a wok over a medium–high heat, then add 1 tablespoon of the oil. Add the asparagus and stir-fry for 1 minute. Tip the beef and marinade into the wok, standing back because it will splutter, and continue stir-frying until the beef is cooked to your taste, about 1½ minutes for medium. Remove the beef and asparagus from the wok and set aside.

Heat the remaining oil in the wok and stir-fry the garlic, ginger and onion for about 1 minute, until the onion is soft. Add the stock, rice wine and oyster sauce and bring to the boil, stirring. Return the beef and asparagus to the wok, along with the noodles. Use 2 forks to mix all the ingredients together and stir around until the noodles are hot. Sprinkle with sesame seeds.

SERVES 4

- 300 g/10½ oz sirloin steak, thinly sliced
- 250 g/9 oz thick egg noodles
- 2 tbsp peanut or corn oil
- 225 g/8 oz fresh asparagus spears, woody ends cut off, chopped
- 2 large garlic cloves, finely chopped
- 1-cm/½-inch piece fresh ginger, finely chopped
- ½ red onion, thinly sliced
- 4 tbsp beef or vegetable stock
- 1½ tbsp Chinese rice wine
- 2–3 tbsp oyster sauce
- toasted sesame seeds, to garnish

marinade
- 1 tbsp light soy sauce
- 1 tsp sesame oil
- 2 tsp rice wine

GINGER BEEF WITH YELLOW PEPPERS

SERVES 4

500 g/1 lb 2 oz beef fillet,
    cut into 2.5-cm/1-inch cubes

2 tsp groundnut oil

2 garlic cloves, crushed

2 tbsp grated fresh ginger

pinch of chilli flakes

2 yellow peppers, deseeded and
    thinly sliced

125 g/4½ oz baby corn

175 g/6 oz mangetout

freshly cooked rice noodles
    drizzled with sesame oil,
    to serve

marinade

2 tbsp soy sauce

2 tsp groundnut oil

1½ tsp caster sugar

1 tsp cornflour

To make the marinade, mix the soy sauce, oil, sugar and cornflour in a bowl. Stir in the beef, then cover with clingfilm and set aside to marinate for 30 minutes.

Heat a wok over a medium–high heat, then add the oil. Add the garlic, ginger and chilli flakes and cook for 30 seconds. Stir in the yellow peppers and baby corn, and stir-fry for 2 minutes. Add the mangetout and cook for a further minute.

Remove the vegetables from the wok. Add the beef and marinade to the wok and stir-fry for 3–4 minutes, or until cooked to taste. Return the vegetables to the wok, mix well and cook until all the ingredients are heated through. Remove from the heat and serve with cooked noodles.

MEAT

MARINATED BEEF WITH VEGETABLES

To make the marinade, mix the sherry, soy sauce, cornflour, sugar, garlic and oil in a bowl. Add the beef to the mixture and cover with clingfilm. Set aside to marinate for 30 minutes, then remove the beef and discard the marinade.

Heat a wok over a medium–high heat, then add 1 tablespoon of the oil. Stir-fry the beef for 2 minutes, until medium–rare. Remove from the wok and set aside.

Combine the cornflour and soy sauce in a bowl and set aside. Pour the remaining 2 tablespoons of oil into the wok, add the broccoli, carrots and mangetout and stir-fry for 2 minutes.

Add the stock, cover the wok and cook for 1 minute. Stir in the spinach, beef and the cornflour mixture. Cook until the juices boil and thicken. Serve with cooked rice or noodles.

SERVES 4

500 g/1 lb 2 oz rump steak, cut into thin strips

3 tbsp sesame oil

½ tbsp cornflour

½ tbsp soy sauce

1 head of broccoli, cut into florets

2 carrots, cut into thin strips

125 g/4 oz mangetout

125 ml/4 fl oz beef stock

250 g/9 oz baby spinach, shredded

freshly cooked plain rice or noodles, to serve

marinade

1 tbsp dry sherry

½ tbsp soy sauce

½ tbsp cornflour

½ tsp caster sugar

2 garlic cloves, finely chopped

1 tbsp sesame oil

BEEF WITH BLACK PEPPER & LIME

Pound the steak with the blunt side of a knife. Slice diagonally across the grain into thin bite-sized pieces and put in a shallow bowl.

Combine the sugar, peppercorns, soy sauce, chilli, garlic and half the lime juice in a bowl, mixing well. Pour over the beef, stirring to coat. Leave to marinate for 1 hour at room temperature, or overnight in the refrigerator.

Arrange the Chinese leaves in a shallow serving dish. Scatter with the red onion slices.

Heat a wok over a high heat, then add the oil. Stir-fry the meat for 3 minutes. Add the fish sauce and the remaining lime juice, and stir-fry for a further minute.

Tip the beef and juices over the Chinese leaves and onion, then scatter over the mint. Garnish with lime wedges and serve immediately with rice.

SERVES 2–3

350 g/12 oz skirt steak

½ tbsp palm sugar or light brown sugar

1 tbsp black peppercorns, crushed

4 tsp soy sauce

1 fresh red bird's eye chilli, deseeded and finely chopped

½ head of garlic, divided into cloves and crushed

2 tbsp lime juice

½ head Chinese leaves, sliced

½ red onion, thinly sliced

1½ tbsp groundnut oil

½ tsp Thai fish sauce

3 tbsp chopped fresh mint

lime wedges, to garnish

freshly cooked plain rice, to serve

BEEF & BOK CHOI STIR-FRY

SERVES 2–3

350 g/12 oz skirt steak

2 tbsp groundnut oil

1 shallot, chopped

2 tsp finely chopped fresh ginger

1 fresh red chilli, deseeded and
thinly sliced

350 g/12 oz bok choi, stalks cut
into 2.5-cm/1-inch squares and
leaves sliced into wide ribbons

1 tbsp cornflour

2 tbsp beef stock or water

3 tbsp chopped fresh coriander

marinade

2 tbsp soy sauce

1½ tbsp Chinese rice wine or dry
sherry

½ tsp sugar

½ tsp pepper

¼ tsp salt

Pound the steak with the blunt side of a knife. Slice diagonally across the grain into thin bite-sized pieces and put in a shallow bowl.

Combine the marinade ingredients in a bowl and pour over the beef, stirring to coat. Leave to marinate for 1 hour at room temperature, or overnight in the refrigerator.

Heat a wok over a medium–high heat, then add the oil. Stir-fry the shallot, ginger and chilli for 1 minute. Increase the heat to high and add the beef and marinade. Stir-fry for 3 minutes. Add the bok choi stalks and stir-fry for 1 minute. Add the leaves and stir-fry for a further minute.

Mix the cornflour and stock to a smooth paste. Add to the wok and stir-fry for 1 minute, until slightly thickened. Transfer to a warmed serving dish and sprinkle with the coriander. Serve immediately.

BEEF WITH MIXED MUSHROOMS

Grind the Szechuan peppers with the salt, using a mortar and pestle. Sprinkle over both sides of the meat, pressing in well. Slice the meat diagonally across the grain into thin bite-sized pieces and set aside.

Rinse the mushrooms and dry with kitchen paper. If using clumping mushrooms, such as enoki and buna shimeji, slice off the root and separate the clump. Slice cremini mushrooms in half.

Mix the cornflour to a paste with 2 tablespoons of the stock. Add the rice wine and soy sauce, mixing well.

Heat a wok over a medium–high heat, then add 1 tablespoon of the oil. Fry the shallot and ginger for 1 minute. Add the garlic and fry for a few seconds, then add the mushrooms and 2 tablespoons of the stock. Stir-fry for 4 minutes. Add the cornflour mixture and the remaining stock. Bring to the boil, stirring, then reduce the heat and simmer for 2 minutes. Transfer to a warmed serving dish.

Clean the wok and heat over a high heat. Add the remaining oil. Add the beef and stir-fry for 3 minutes. Add to the mushroom mixture and sprinkle with the coriander. Serve immediately.

SERVES 2–3

1½ tbsp Szechuan peppers

½ tsp salt

350 g/12 oz sirloin or rump steak

200 g/7 oz mixed small mushrooms, such as cremini, enoki and buna shimeji

½ tbsp cornflour

125 ml/4 fl oz Spicy Beef Stock (see page 16) or beef stock

2 tsp Chinese rice wine or dry sherry

4 tsp soy sauce

3 tbsp groundnut oil

1 shallot, finely chopped

1 tsp finely chopped fresh ginger

1 large garlic clove, thinly sliced

3 tbsp chopped fresh coriander, to garnish

SPICY SZECHUAN PORK

Bring a saucepan of water to the boil and place the pork slices in the pan, then cover and simmer for about 20 minutes, skimming occasionally. Leave the pork to cool and rest.

Heat a wok over a medium–high heat, then add the oil. Stir-fry the pork slices until they begin to shrink. Stir in the chilli bean sauce, then add the black beans and the red bean paste, if using. Finally, toss in the green and red peppers and the remaining ingredients and stir-fry for a couple of minutes, or until the peppers have softened. Serve immediately with rice.

SERVES 4

280 g/10 oz pork belly, thinly sliced

1 tbsp vegetable or groundnut oil

1 tbsp chilli bean sauce

1 tbsp fermented black beans, rinsed and lightly mashed

1 tsp sweet red bean paste (optional)

1 green pepper, deseeded and finely sliced

1 red pepper, deseeded and finely sliced

1 tsp sugar

1 tsp dark soy sauce

pinch of white pepper

freshly cooked plain rice, to serve

PAD THAI

SERVES 4

225 g/8 oz thick rice noodles

2 tbsp vegetable or groundnut oil

2 garlic cloves, chopped

2 fresh red chillies, deseeded and chopped

175 g/6 oz pork fillet, thinly sliced

115 g/4 oz raw prawns, peeled, deveined and chopped

8 fresh Chinese chives, snipped

2 tbsp Thai fish sauce

juice of 1 lime

2 tsp palm sugar or light brown sugar

2 eggs, beaten

115 g/4 oz fresh beansprouts

4 tbsp chopped fresh coriander, plus extra sprigs to garnish

115 g/4 oz unsalted peanuts, chopped, plus extra to serve

Soak the noodles in enough lukewarm water to cover for 15 minutes, or cook according to the instructions on the packet, until soft. Drain well and set aside.

Heat a wok over a medium–high heat, then add the oil. Stir-fry the garlic, chillies and pork for 2–3 minutes. Add the prawns and stir-fry for a further 2–3 minutes.

Add the chives and noodles, then cover and cook for 1–2 minutes. Add the fish sauce, lime juice, sugar and eggs. Cook, stirring and tossing constantly to mix in the eggs.

Stir in the beansprouts, coriander and peanuts and mix well, then transfer to serving dishes. Scatter over some extra peanuts and serve immediately, garnished with coriander sprigs.

PORK STIR FRY WITH CASHEWS, LIME & MINT

Diagonally slice the pork across the grain into thin bite-sized pieces. Flatten with the back of a knife blade and spread out on a plate. Using a mortar and pestle, crush the coriander seeds, peppercorns, salt, sugar and lime rind together. Spread the mixture over both sides of the pork, pressing it in well. Leave to stand for 15 minutes.

Heat a wok over a high heat, then add 1 tablespoon of the oil. Stir-fry the pork for 2–3 minutes, until no longer pink. Transfer to a plate with the juices. Wipe the wok clean with kitchen paper.

Heat the wok over a medium–high heat, then add the remaining oil. Stir-fry the ginger and garlic for a few seconds. Add the white spring onion and green pepper, and stir-fry for 2 minutes. Add the cashew nuts and salt, then stir-fry for a further minute.

Increase the heat to high, then return the pork and juices to the wok. Add the stock, lime juice, fish sauce and the green spring onion. Stir-fry for 30 seconds to heat through, then sprinkle with the mint and serve.

SERVES 2

280 g/10 oz pork fillet

1 tsp coriander seeds

½ tsp white peppercorns

¼ tsp salt

¼ tsp sugar

juice and finely grated rind of 1 lime

2 tbsp groundnut oil

1 tsp finely chopped fresh ginger

1 garlic clove, thinly sliced

3 spring onions, white and green parts separated, then halved lengthways and sliced into 2-cm/¾-inch pieces

1 small green pepper, deseeded and thinly sliced

2 tbsp cashew nuts, roughly chopped

large pinch of salt

1 tbsp chicken stock

1 tsp Thai fish sauce

2 tbsp roughly chopped fresh mint, to garnish

PORK BELLY ON CHINESE LEAVES

Using the tip of a very sharp knife, score the pork rind at 1-cm/½-inch intervals. Combine the marinade ingredients, pour the mixture into a dish and add the pork, rubbing the marinade into the slashes. Leave to stand at room temperature for 1 hour, turning occasionally.

Preheat the oven to 220°C/425°F/Gas Mark 7. Line a small roasting tin with foil and put a rack in it. Reserving the marinade, place the pork on the rack and put the tin on the top shelf of the oven. Roast for 15 minutes, then reduce the oven temperature to 180°C/350°F/Gas Mark 4. Turn the pork over and brush with the marinade. Roast for 20 minutes, then turn, brush with the marinade again and roast for a further 20 minutes. Remove from the oven and leave to cool. Diagonally slice the pork into 1-cm/½-inch pieces. Put in a bowl and mix with the remaining marinade.

Heat a wok over a high heat, then add 1 tablespoon of the oil. Add the pork slices and marinade, and stir-fry for 2 minutes, until the marinade is reduced and bubbling. Pour in the stock, scraping up any sediment. Stir-fry for 2 minutes, until reduced. Remove from the wok and keep warm. Wipe the wok clean with kitchen paper.

Heat the wok over a high heat, then add the remaining oil. Add the ginger and stir-fry for a few seconds. Add the Chinese leaves, spring onions, sugar and salt, and stir-fry for 1 minute, until just cooked and still brightly coloured.

Transfer the vegetables to a warmed serving dish. Pour the pork and juices over the top and serve immediately.

SERVES 2

- 4 strips boneless pork belly, about 650 g/1 lb 7 oz in total
- 2 tbsp groundnut oil
- 6 tbsp Basic Chinese Stock (see page 16) or chicken stock
- 1 thin slice fresh ginger
- ½ head Chinese leaves, sliced diagonally into ribbons
- 6 spring onions, green parts included, sliced diagonally into 4-cm/1½-inch pieces
- ½ tsp sugar
- ¼ tsp salt

marinade

- 2 tbsp sugar
- 2 tbsp Chinese rice wine or dry sherry
- 1 tbsp soy sauce
- 4-cm/1½-inch piece fresh ginger, roughly chopped and squeezed in a garlic press
- ½ tsp salt
- ¼ tsp Chinese five-spice
- 4 tbsp hoisin sauce

PORK, CARROT & GINGER STIR FRY

SERVES 2

250 g/9 oz pork fillet

2 tbsp groundnut oil

2 large garlic cloves, thinly sliced

1 fresh green chilli, deseeded and thinly sliced diagonally

6 carrots, cut into thin strips

50 g/1¾ oz fresh ginger, cut into thin strips

140 g/5 oz canned bamboo shoots, drained

1½ tsp Szechuan peppers, crushed

100 ml/3½ fl oz Basic Chinese Stock (see page 16) or chicken stock

2 tbsp light soy sauce

marinade

2 tsp Chinese rice wine or dry sherry

2 tsp light soy sauce

½ tsp sugar

¼ tsp salt

Diagonally slice the pork across the grain very thinly, then cut into 4-cm/1½-inch lengths. Put in a bowl. Combine the marinade ingredients and pour over the pork. Leave to stand for 30 minutes.

Heat a wok over a medium heat, then add the oil. Stir-fry the garlic and chilli for 30 seconds, or until the garlic just starts to colour.

Add the pork and marinade, and increase the heat to high. Stir-fry for 1 minute, then add the carrots, ginger, bamboo shoots and Szechuan peppers. Stir-fry for a further minute, then pour in the stock and soy sauce. Stir-fry for 4–5 minutes, until the sauce has reduced slightly. Transfer to a warmed dish and serve immediately.

MEAT

SINGAPORE NOODLES

Soak the noodles in enough lukewarm water to cover for 15 minutes, or cook according to the packet instructions, until soft. Drain and set aside. Meanwhile, put the curry paste and turmeric in a small bowl and stir in 4 tablespoons of the water, then set aside.

Heat a wok over a high heat, then add the oil. Add the onion and garlic and stir-fry for 1 minute, or until the onion softens. Add the broccoli and beans to the wok with the remaining water and continue stir-frying for 2 minutes. Add the pork and stir-fry for a further minute. Add the prawns, Chinese leaves and chilli to the wok and continue stir-frying for a further 2 minutes, until the meat is cooked through and the vegetables are tender, but still with a little bite. Scoop out of the wok and keep warm.

Add the spring onions, noodles and curry paste mixture to the wok. Use 2 forks to mix together the noodles and onions, and continue stir-frying for about 2 minutes, until the noodles are hot and have picked up a dark golden colour from the turmeric. Return the other ingredients to the wok and continue stir-frying and mixing for 1 minute. Garnish with fresh coriander sprigs and serve.

SERVES 4

200 g/7 oz fine rice noodles

1 tbsp mild, medium or hot curry paste, to taste

1 tsp ground turmeric

6 tbsp water

2 tbsp groundnut or corn oil

½ onion, very thinly sliced

2 large garlic cloves, thinly sliced

85 g/3 oz broccoli, cut into very small florets

85 g/3 oz green beans, cut into 2.5-cm/1-inch lengths

85 g/3 oz pork fillet, cut into thin strips

85 g/3 oz small cooked peeled prawns, thawed if frozen

55 g/2 oz Chinese leaves or romaine lettuce, thinly shredded

1 fresh bird's eye chilli, deseeded and thinly sliced

2 spring onions, white parts only, thinly shredded

fresh coriander sprigs, to garnish

HOISIN PORK WITH GARLIC NOODLES

Cook the noodles in a saucepan of boiling water for 4 minutes, or according to the packet instructions, until soft. Drain well, rinse under cold running water and drain again, then set aside.

Sprinkle the pork with the sugar and use your hands to toss together. Heat a wok over a high heat, then add the oil. Add the pork and stir-fry for about 3 minutes, until the pork is cooked through and is no longer pink. Use a slotted spoon to remove the pork from the wok and keep warm. Add both vinegars to the wok and boil until they are reduced to about 5 tablespoons. Pour in the hoisin sauce with the spring onions and let bubble until reduced by half. Add to the pork and stir together.

Quickly wipe out the wok with kitchen paper and reheat. Add the garlic-flavoured oil and heat, then add the garlic slices and stir around for about 30 seconds, until they are golden and crisp. Use a slotted spoon to scoop them out of the wok and set aside.

Add the noodles to the wok and stir to warm through. Divide the noodles among 4 serving dishes, top with the pork and spring onion mixture and sprinkle with the garlic slices.

SERVES 4

250 g/9 oz thick egg noodles

450 g/1 lb pork fillet, thinly sliced

1 tsp sugar

1 tbsp groundnut or corn oil

4 tbsp rice vinegar

4 tbsp white wine vinegar

4 tbsp hoisin sauce

2 spring onions, diagonally sliced

about 2 tbsp garlic-flavoured corn oil

2 large garlic cloves, thinly sliced

ANTS CLIMBING A TREE

SERVES 4

250 g/9 oz thick rice noodles

1 tbsp cornflour

3 tbsp soy sauce

1½ tbsp Chinese rice wine

1½ tsp sugar

1½ tsp sesame oil

350 g/12 oz lean fresh pork mince

1½ tbsp groundnut oil

2 large garlic cloves, finely
   chopped

1 large fresh red chilli, or to taste,
   deseeded and thinly sliced

3 spring onions, finely chopped

finely chopped fresh coriander,
   to garnish

Soak the noodles in enough lukewarm water to cover for
15 minutes, or cook according to the packet instructions, until
soft. Drain well and set aside.

Meanwhile, put the cornflour in a separate large bowl, then
stir in the soy sauce, rice wine, sugar and sesame oil, stirring
until smooth. Add the pork mince and use your hands to toss the
ingredients together without squeezing the pork. Set aside to
marinate for 10 minutes.

Heat a wok over a high heat, then add the groundnut oil.
Add the garlic, chilli and spring onions and stir around for about
30 seconds. Tip in the pork mince together with any marinade left
in the bowl and stir-fry for about 5 minutes, or until the pork is
no longer pink. Add the noodles and use 2 forks to mix together.
Sprinkle with the chopped coriander and serve.

JAPANESE-STYLE PORK

Diagonally slice the pork across the grain very thinly, then cut into 4-cm/1½-inch lengths. Put in a bowl. Combine the marinade ingredients, stirring well to mix in the honey, and pour over the pork. Leave to stand for 1 hour at room temperature, or overnight in the refrigerator. Drain the pork in a sieve set over a bowl, reserving the marinade.

Heat a wok over a medium heat, then add the groundnut oil. Stir-fry the garlic for a few seconds, then add the beans and stir-fry for 1 minute. Add the pork and marinade, and increase the heat to high. Season to taste with salt and pepper, and stir-fry for 4–5 minutes, or until the beans are tender and the pork is cooked through.

Sprinkle with the sesame seeds pour in the oil, then fry for a further 30 seconds. Transfer to a warmed serving dish and serve immediately.

SERVES 2

280 g/10 oz pork fillet

2 tbsp groundnut oil

1 garlic clove, thinly sliced

115 g/4 oz French beans, trimmed and sliced into 4-cm/1½-inch lengths

1½ tsp sesame seeds

½ tsp sesame oil

salt and pepper

marinade

3 tbsp shoyu or tamari (Japanese soy sauce)

3 tbsp mirin

finely grated rind and juice of ½ orange

1 tbsp clear honey

½ –1 fresh red chilli, deseeded and finely chopped

1 tsp finely chopped fresh ginger

¼ tsp salt

STIR-FRIED LAMB WITH ORANGE

Heat a wok, without adding any oil. Add the lamb mince and dry-fry for 5 minutes, or until evenly browned. Drain away any excess fat from the wok.

Add the garlic, cumin seeds, coriander and red onion to the wok and stir-fry for a further 5 minutes.

Stir in the orange rind and juice and the soy sauce, mixing until thoroughly combined. Cover, reduce the heat and leave to simmer, stirring occasionally, for 15 minutes.

Remove the lid, increase the heat and add the orange segments. Stir to mix.

Season to taste with salt and pepper and heat through for a further 2–3 minutes. Transfer the stir-fry to warmed serving dishes and garnish with snipped chives and strips of orange zest. Serve immediately.

SERVES 4

450 g/1 lb fresh lamb mince

2 garlic cloves, crushed

1 tsp cumin seeds

1 tsp ground coriander

1 red onion, sliced

finely grated rind and juice of
    1 orange

2 tbsp soy sauce

1 orange, peeled and segmented

salt and pepper

snipped fresh chives and strips of
    orange zest, to garnish

LAMB WITH BLACK BEAN SAUCE

SERVES 4

450 g/1 lb lamb neck fillet or boneless leg of lamb

1 egg white, lightly beaten

4 tbsp cornflour

1 tsp Chinese five-spice

3 tbsp sunflower oil

1 red onion, sliced

1 red pepper, deseeded and sliced

1 green pepper, deseeded and sliced

1 yellow or orange pepper, deseeded and sliced

5 tbsp black bean sauce

freshly cooked noodles, to serve

Using a sharp knife, slice the lamb into very thin strips.

Mix together the egg white, cornflour and Chinese five-spice. Toss the lamb strips in the mixture until evenly coated.

Heat a wok over a high heat, then add the oil. Stir-fry the lamb for 5 minutes, or until it crispens around the edges.

Add the onion and pepper slices to the wok and stir-fry for 5–6 minutes, or until the vegetables just begin to soften.

Stir the black bean sauce into the mixture in the wok and heat through.

Transfer the lamb and sauce to warmed serving dishes and serve with cooked noodles.

MEAT

157

RED LAMB CURRY

Heat a wok over a high heat, then add the oil. Add the onion and garlic and stir-fry for 2–3 minutes, until softened. Add the lamb and stir-fry the mixture quickly until lightly browned.

Stir in the curry paste and cook for a few seconds, then add the coconut milk and sugar and bring to the boil. Reduce the heat and simmer for 15 minutes, stirring occasionally.

Stir in the red pepper, stock, fish sauce and lime juice, then cover and simmer for a further 15 minutes, or until the lamb is tender.

Add the water chestnuts, coriander and chopped basil and season to taste with salt and pepper. Transfer to serving plates, then garnish with basil leaves and serve with rice.

SERVES 4

2 tbsp vegetable oil

1 large onion, sliced

2 garlic cloves, crushed

500 g/1 lb 2 oz lean boneless leg of lamb, cut into 3-cm/1¼-inch cubes

2 tbsp Thai red curry paste

150 ml/5 fl oz coconut milk

1 tbsp light brown sugar

1 large red pepper, deseeded and thickly sliced

150 ml/5 fl oz lamb or beef stock

1 tbsp Thai fish sauce

2 tbsp lime juice

225 g/8 oz canned water chestnuts, drained

2 tbsp chopped fresh coriander

2 tbsp chopped fresh basil, plus extra leaves to garnish

salt and pepper

freshly cooked jasmine rice, to serve

LAMB & LEEK
STIR FRY

Diagonally slice the lamb across the grain into thin bite-sized pieces. Flatten with the back of a knife blade and put in a bowl. Combine the garlic, soy sauce, rice wine, sugar and salt. Pour the mixture over the lamb. Leave to stand for 1 hour at room temperature, or overnight in the refrigerator.

Mix the cornflour to a thin paste with the Spicy Beef Stock. Heat a wok over a high heat, then add 1 tablespoon of the oil. Add the lamb and stir-fry for 1 minute, then season to taste with pepper. Add the cornflour paste and stir-fry for a further minute. Remove from the wok and keep warm. Wipe the wok clean with kitchen paper.

Heat the wok over a high heat, the add the remaining oil. Add the leeks and chicken stock, and stir-fry for 2 minutes, until just cooked and still bright green and crisp. Return the lamb to the wok and stir-fry for 30 seconds. Transfer to a warmed serving dish and serve immediately.

SERVES 2

280 g/10 oz lamb neck fillet

1 garlic clove, finely chopped

2 tsp soy sauce

2 tsp Chinese rice wine or dry sherry

½ tsp sugar

¼ tsp salt

½ tbsp cornflour

Basic Chinese Stock (see page 16) or chicken stock

2 tbsp groundnut oil

3 leeks, green part included, sliced into 4-cm/1½-inch pieces

1 tbsp chicken stock or water

pepper

XINJIANG LAMB CASSEROLE

SERVES 5–6

1–2 tbsp vegetable or
  groundnut oil

400 g/14 oz lamb or mutton,
  cut into bite-sized cubes

1 onion, roughly chopped

1 green pepper, deseeded and
  roughly chopped

1 carrot, roughly chopped

1 turnip, roughly chopped

2 tomatoes, roughly chopped

2.5-cm/1-inch piece fresh ginger,
  thinly sliced

300 ml/10 fl oz water

1 tsp salt

Heat a wok over a high heat, then add the oil. Stir-fry the lamb
for 1–2 minutes, or until the meat is sealed on all sides.

Transfer the meat to a large flameproof casserole and add all
the other ingredients. Bring to the boil, then cover and simmer
over a low heat for 35 minutes, until the lamb and vegetables are
tender. Serve immediately.

LAMB WITH LIME LEAVES

Using a sharp knife, cut the lamb into thin strips or cubes. Heat a wok over a high heat, then add the oil. Add the chillies, garlic, shallots, lemon grass, kaffir lime leaves, tamarind paste and sugar.

Add the lamb to the wok and stir-fry for 5 minutes, tossing well so that the lamb is evenly coated in the spice mixture.

Pour the coconut milk into the wok and bring to the boil. Reduce the heat and simmer for 20 minutes.

Add the cherry tomatoes and chopped coriander to the wok and simmer for 5 minutes. Transfer to serving plates and serve with rice.

SERVES 4

450 g/1 lb lean boneless lamb (leg or loin fillet)

2 tbsp groundnut oil

2 fresh bird's eye chillies, deseeded and finely chopped

2 garlic cloves, crushed

4 shallots, chopped

2 lemon grass stems, sliced

6 fresh kaffir lime leaves

1 tbsp tamarind paste

2 tbsp palm sugar or light brown sugar

300 ml/10 fl oz coconut milk

175 g/6 oz cherry tomatoes, halved

1 tbsp chopped fresh coriander

freshly cooked Thai fragrant rice, to serve

POULTRY

SWEET & SOUR CHICKEN

Combine all the marinade ingredients in a bowl and marinate the chicken for at least 20 minutes.

To prepare the sauce, heat the vinegar in a pan and add the sugar, soy sauce and tomato ketchup. Stir to dissolve the sugar, then set aside.

Heat a wok over a high heat, then add 3 tablespoons of the vegetable oil. Stir-fry the chicken until it starts to turn golden brown. Remove and set aside. Wipe the wok clean with kitchen paper.

Heat the wok over a high heat, and add the remaining vegetable oil and cook the garlic and ginger until fragrant. Add the vegetables and cook for 2 minutes. Add the chicken and cook for 1 minute. Finally, add the sauce and the sesame oil, then stir in the spring onion and serve immediately with rice.

SERVES 4–6

450 g/1 lb lean chicken, cubed

5 tbsp vegetable or groundnut oil

½ tsp crushed garlic

½ tsp finely chopped fresh ginger

1 green pepper, deseeded and roughly chopped

1 onion, roughly chopped

1 carrot, finely sliced

1 tsp sesame oil

1 tbsp finely chopped spring onion

freshly cooked plain rice, to serve

marinade

2 tsp light soy sauce

1 tsp Chinese rice wine

pinch of white pepper

½ tsp salt

dash of sesame oil

sauce

8 tbsp rice vinegar

4 tbsp sugar

2 tsp light soy sauce

6 tbsp tomato ketchup

GONG BAU
CHICKEN

Combine all the marinade ingredients in a bowl and marinate the chicken, covered, for at least 20 minutes. Combine all the ingredients for the sauce and set aside.

Heat a wok over a high heat, then add the vegetable oil. Stir-fry the chillies and peppers until crisp and fragrant. Toss in the chicken pieces. When they begin to turn white, add the garlic, ginger and spring onion. Stir-fry for about 5 minutes, or until the chicken is cooked through.

Pour in the sauce and mix together thoroughly, then stir in the peanuts. Serve immediately with rice.

SERVES 4

2 skinless, boneless chicken breasts, cut into cubes

1 tbsp vegetable or groundnut oil

10 dried red chillies, or to taste, each snipped into 2–3 pieces

1 tsp Szechuan peppers

3 garlic cloves, finely sliced

2.5-cm/1-inch piece fresh ginger, finely sliced

1 tbsp finely chopped spring onion

85 g/3 oz roasted peanuts

freshly cooked plain rice, to serve

marinade

2 tsp light soy sauce

1 tsp Chinese rice wine

½ tsp sugar

sauce

1 tsp light soy sauce

1 tsp dark soy sauce

1 tsp black rice vinegar

a few drops of sesame oil

2 tbsp chicken stock

1 tsp sugar

CHICKEN WITH CASHEW NUTS

SERVES 4–6

450 g/1 lb skinless, boneless chicken breasts, cut into bite-sized pieces

2 dried Chinese mushrooms, soaked in warm water for 20 minutes

2 tbsp vegetable or groundnut oil

4 slices fresh ginger

1 tsp finely chopped garlic

1 red pepper, deseeded and cut into 2.5-cm/1-inch squares

1 tbsp light soy sauce

85 g/3 oz roasted cashew nuts

marinade

1 tsp Chinese rice wine

pinch of sugar

½ tsp salt

2 tbsp light soy sauce

Combine all the marinade ingredients in a bowl and marinate the chicken for at least 20 minutes.

Squeeze any excess water from the mushrooms and finely slice, discarding any tough stems. Reserve the soaking water.

Heat a wok over a medium–high heat, then add 1 tablespoon of the oil. Add the ginger and stir-fry until fragrant. Stir in the chicken and cook for 2 minutes, or until it begins to turn brown. Before the chicken is cooked through, remove and set aside. Wipe the wok clean with kitchen paper.

Heat the wok over a medium–high heat, then add the remaining oil. Stir-fry the garlic until fragrant. Add the mushrooms and red pepper and stir-fry for 1 minute. Add about 2 tablespoons of the mushroom-soaking water and cook for about 2 minutes, or until the water has evaporated.

Return the chicken to the wok, then add the soy sauce and cashew nuts and stir-fry for 2 minutes, or until the chicken is cooked through.

CHICKEN & PEANUT CURRY

Heat a wok over a medium–high heat, then add the oil. Stir-fry the onions for 1 minute. Add the curry paste and stir-fry for 1–2 minutes.

Pour in the coconut milk and stock. Add the lime leaves and lemon grass and simmer for 1 minute. Add the chicken and gradually bring to the boil. Simmer for 8–10 minutes, until the chicken is tender.

Stir in the fish sauce, soy sauce and sugar and simmer for 1–2 minutes. Stir in the peanuts, pineapple and cucumber and cook for 30 seconds. Serve immediately with extra peanuts and cucumber on the side.

SERVES 4

- 1 tbsp vegetable or groundnut oil
- 2 red onions, sliced
- 2 tbsp Penang curry paste
- 400 ml/14 fl oz coconut milk
- 150 ml/5 fl oz chicken stock
- 4 kaffir lime leaves, roughly torn
- 1 lemon grass stem, finely chopped
- 6 skinless, boneless chicken thighs, chopped
- 1 tbsp Thai fish sauce
- 2 tbsp Thai soy sauce
- 1 tsp palm sugar or light brown sugar
- 50 g/1¾ oz unsalted roasted peanuts, chopped, plus extra to serve
- 175 g/6 oz fresh pineapple, chopped coarsely
- 15-cm/6-inch piece cucumber, peeled and halved lengthways, then deseeded and sliced, plus extra to serve

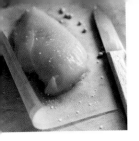

CHICKEN CHOW MEIN

Cook the noodles in a saucepan of boiling water for 4 minutes, or according to the instructions on the packet, until soft. Drain and set aside.

Heat a wok over a medium heat, then add the sunflower oil. Add the chicken, garlic, red pepper, mushrooms, spring onions and beansprouts to the wok and stir-fry for about 5 minutes.

Add the noodles to the wok, toss well and stir-fry for a further 5 minutes. Drizzle over the soy sauce and sesame oil and toss until thoroughly combined.

Transfer to warmed serving dishes and serve immediately.

SERVES 4

250 g/9 oz medium egg noodles

2 tbsp sunflower oil

280 g/10 oz cooked chicken breasts, shredded

1 garlic clove, finely chopped

1 red pepper, deseeded and thinly sliced

100 g/3½ oz shiitake mushrooms, sliced

6 spring onions, sliced

100 g/3½ oz fresh beansprouts

3 tbsp soy sauce

1 tbsp sesame oil

THAI GREEN CHICKEN CURRY

SERVES 4

1 tbsp vegetable or groundnut oil

1 onion, sliced

1 garlic clove, finely chopped

2–3 tbsp Thai green curry paste

400 ml/14 fl oz coconut milk

150 ml/5 fl oz chicken stock

4 kaffir lime leaves

4 skinless, boneless chicken
  breasts, cut into cubes

1 tbsp Thai fish sauce

2 tbsp Thai soy sauce

grated rind and juice of ½ lime

1 tsp soft light brown sugar

4 tbsp chopped fresh coriander,
  to garnish

freshly cooked jasmine rice,
  to serve

Heat a wok over a medium–high heat, then add the oil. Stir-fry the onion and garlic for 1–2 minutes, until starting to soften. Add the curry paste and stir-fry for 1–2 minutes.

Add the coconut milk, stock and lime leaves, bring to the boil and add the chicken. Reduce the heat and simmer gently for 15–20 minutes, until the chicken is tender.

Add the fish sauce, soy sauce, lime rind and juice and sugar. Cook for 2–3 minutes, until the sugar has dissolved. Garnish with chopped coriander and serve immediately with rice.

THAI RED CHICKEN CURRY

Place the garlic, chillies, lemon grass, lime rind, lime leaves, curry paste and coriander seeds in a food processor and process until the mixture is smooth.

Heat a wok over a medium–high heat, then add the oil. Add the chicken and the garlic mixture and stir-fry for 5 minutes. Add the coconut milk, stock and soy sauce and bring to the boil. Reduce the heat and cook, stirring, for a further 3 minutes. Stir in the ground peanuts and simmer for 20 minutes.

Add the spring onions, red pepper and aubergines and simmer, stirring occasionally, for a further 10 minutes. Remove from the heat and stir in the coriander. Serve immediately with jasmine rice, garnished with extra coriander.

SERVES 4

6 garlic cloves, chopped

2 fresh red chillies, chopped

2 tbsp chopped fresh lemon grass

1 tsp finely grated lime rind

1 tbsp chopped fresh kaffir lime leaves

1 tbsp Thai red curry paste

1 tbsp coriander seeds, toasted and crushed

1 tbsp chilli oil

4 skinless, boneless chicken breasts, sliced

300 ml/10 fl oz coconut milk

300 ml/10 fl oz chicken stock

1 tbsp soy sauce

55 g/2 oz unsalted peanuts, toasted and ground

3 spring onions, diagonally sliced

1 red pepper, deseeded and sliced

3 Thai aubergines, sliced

2 tbsp chopped fresh coriander, plus extra to garnish

freshly cooked jasmine rice, to serve

CHICKEN FRIED RICE

Heat a wok over a medium heat, then add the oil. Add the shallots and cook until soft, then add the chicken and 2 tablespoons of the soy sauce and stir-fry for 5–6 minutes.

Stir in the carrots, celery, red pepper, peas and sweetcorn and stir-fry for a further 5 minutes. Add the rice and stir thoroughly.

Finally, stir in the scrambled eggs and the remaining soy sauce. Serve immediately.

SERVES 4

½ tbsp sesame oil

6 shallots, peeled and cut into quarters

450 g/1 lb cooked chicken, cubed

3 tbsp soy sauce

2 carrots, diced

1 celery stick, diced

1 red pepper, deseeded and diced

175 g/6 oz fresh peas

100 g/3½ oz canned sweetcorn, drained

275 g/9¾ oz cooked long-grain rice

2 large eggs, scrambled

EGG FRIED RICE
WITH CHICKEN

SERVES 4

225 g/8 oz jasmine rice

3 skinless, boneless chicken
breasts, cut into cubes

400 ml/14 fl oz coconut milk

50 g/1¾ oz creamed coconut,
chopped

2–3 coriander roots, chopped

thinly pared rind of 1 lemon

1 fresh green chilli, deseeded and
chopped

3 fresh Thai basil leaves

1 tbsp Thai fish sauce

1 tbsp oil

3 eggs, beaten

fresh chives, to garnish

fresh coriander sprigs, to garnish

Cook the rice in a saucepan of boiling water for 12–15 minutes.
Drain well, then leave to cool and chill overnight.

Put the chicken into a saucepan and cover with the coconut
milk. Add the creamed coconut, coriander roots, lemon rind and
chilli, and bring to the boil. Simmer for 8–10 minutes, until the
chicken is tender. Remove from the heat. Stir in the basil and
fish sauce.

Meanwhile, heat a wok over a medium–high heat, then add the
oil. Stir-fry the rice for 2–3 minutes. Pour in the eggs and stir until
they have cooked and are thoroughly mixed with the rice.

Line 4 small ovenproof bowls or ramekins with clingfilm and
pack with the rice. Turn out carefully onto serving plates and
remove the clingfilm. Serve with the chicken mixture and garnish
with chives and coriander sprigs.

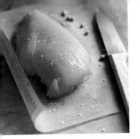

PEPPERED CHICKEN STIR FRY

In a small bowl, combine half the soy sauce, the cornflour, rice wine and salt.

Put the chicken pieces in a shallow dish and pour over the soy sauce mixture, stirring to coat. Leave to stand for 15 minutes.

Mix the remaining soy sauce with the stock and oyster sauce, and set aside.

Heat a wok over a high heat, then add the oil. Add the chicken and stir-fry for 3 minutes, until no longer pink. Remove from the wok with a slotted spoon and drain on kitchen paper.

Reduce the heat slightly, then add the ginger, garlic, white spring onion and the crushed peppercorns, and stir for a few seconds. Add the baby corn, red pepper and water chestnuts. Stir-fry for 2 minutes, then return the chicken to the wok. Add the mangetout and the soy sauce mixture, and stir-fry for 1–2 minutes, until the sauce is thickened.

Sprinkle with the sliced green spring onion and cook for a few more seconds. Serve immediately.

SERVES 4–6

4 tsp soy sauce

1 tbsp cornflour

1 tbsp Chinese rice wine or dry sherry

¼ tsp salt

350 g/12 oz skinless, boneless chicken breasts, cut into cubes

6 tbsp Basic Chinese Stock (see page 16) or chicken stock

1 tbsp oyster sauce

4 tbsp groundnut oil

1 tsp finely chopped fresh ginger

1 large garlic clove, thinly sliced

4 spring onions, white and green parts separated, diagonally sliced into 2-cm/¾-inch pieces

½ tbsp white peppercorns, crushed

8 baby corn, halved diagonally

½ small red pepper, deseeded and thinly sliced

140 g/5 oz canned water chestnuts, drained

115 g/4 oz mangetout, halved diagonally

GINGER CHICKEN WITH SESAME SEEDS

Combine the marinade ingredients in a bowl. Add the chicken and toss to coat well. Cover with clingfilm and chill in the refrigerator for 1 hour.

Remove the chicken from the marinade with a slotted spoon. Heat a wok over a medium–high heat, then add the oil. Stir-fry the chicken and leek until the chicken is browned and the leek is beginning to soften. Stir in the remaining vegetables, the ginger and wine. Reduce the heat, cover and simmer for 5 minutes.

Place the sesame seeds on a baking tray under a hot grill. Stir them once to make sure they toast evenly. Set aside to cool.

In a small bowl, combine the cornflour with the water and mix until smooth. Gradually add the liquid to the wok, stirring constantly until thickened.

Sprinkle with the sesame seeds and serve immediately.

SERVES 4

500 g/1 lb 2 oz skinless, boneless chicken breasts, cut into strips

2 tbsp groundnut oil

1 leek, thinly sliced

1 head of broccoli, cut into small florets

2 carrots, thinly sliced

½ cauliflower, cut into small florets

1 tsp grated fresh ginger

5 tbsp white wine

2 tbsp sesame seeds

1 tbsp cornflour

1 tbsp water

marinade

4 tbsp soy sauce

4 tbsp water

CHICKEN & GREEN VEGETABLES

SERVES 4

250 g/9 oz medium egg noodles

2 tbsp groundnut or corn oil

1 large garlic clove, crushed

1 fresh green chilli, deseeded and sliced

1 tbsp Chinese five-spice

2 skinless, boneless chicken breasts, cut into thin strips

2 green peppers, deseeded and sliced

115 g/4 oz head of broccoli, cut into small florets

55 g/2 oz French beans, cut into 4-cm/1½-inch pieces

5 tbsp vegetable or chicken stock

2 tbsp oyster sauce

2 tbsp soy sauce

1 tbsp Chinese rice wine or dry sherry

100 g/3½ oz fresh beansprouts

Cook the noodles in a saucepan of boiling water for 4 minutes, or according to the packet instructions, until soft. Drain, rinse and drain again, then set aside.

Heat a wok over a high heat, then add 1 tablespoon of the oil. Add the garlic, chilli and five-spice and stir-fry for about 30 seconds. Add the chicken and stir-fry for 3 minutes, or until it is cooked through. Use a slotted spoon to remove the chicken from the wok and set aside.

Add the remaining oil to the wok and heat. Add the green peppers, broccoli and beans and stir-fry for about 2 minutes. Stir in the stock, oyster sauce, soy sauce and rice wine and return the chicken to the wok. Continue stir-frying for about 1 minute, until the chicken is warmed through and the vegetables are tender but still firm to the bite. Add the noodles and beansprouts and use 2 forks to mix all the ingredients together. Serve immediately.

SWEET & SOUR NOODLES WITH CHICKEN

Cook the noodles in a large saucepan of boiling water for 4 minutes, or according to the packet instructions, until soft. Drain, rinse and drain again, then set aside.

Meanwhile, to make the sauce, stir half the water into the arrowroot and set aside. Mix together the remaining sauce ingredients and the remaining water in a small saucepan and bring to the boil. Stir in the arrowroot mixture and continue boiling until the sauce becomes clear, glossy and thick. Remove from the heat and set aside.

Heat a wok over a high heat, then add the oil. Add the onion and stir-fry for 1 minute. Stir in the chicken, carrot and red pepper and continue stir-frying for about 3 minutes, or until the chicken is cooked through. Add the bamboo shoots and cashew nuts and stir them around to brown the nuts lightly.

Stir the sauce into the wok and heat until it starts to bubble. Add the noodles and use 2 forks to mix them with the chicken and vegetables. Serve immediately.

SERVES 4

250 g/9 oz medium egg noodles

2 tbsp groundnut or corn oil

1 onion, thinly sliced

4 skinless, bonless chicken thighs, cut into thin strips

1 carrot, cut into thin half-moon slices

1 red pepper, deseeded and finely chopped

100 g/3½ oz canned bamboo shoots, drained weight

55 g/2 oz cashew nuts

sweet & sour sauce

125 ml/4 fl oz water

1½ tsp arrowroot

4 tbsp rice vinegar

3 tbsp light brown sugar

2 tsp dark soy sauce

2 tsp tomato purée

2 large garlic cloves, very finely chopped

1-cm/½-inch piece fresh ginger, very finely chopped

pinch of salt

YAKI SOBA

Cook the noodles according to the instructions on the packet. Drain well, and tip into a bowl.

Mix the onion, beansprouts, red pepper, chicken and prawns together in a separate bowl. Stir through the noodles.

Heat a wok over a high heat, then add the groundnut oil. Add the noodle mixture and stir-fry for 4 minutes, or until golden, then add the shoyu, mirin and sesame oil and toss together.

Divide the mixture between 2 bowls, sprinkle with the sesame seeds and spring onions and serve immediately.

SERVES 2

400 g/14 oz ramen noodles

1 onion, finely sliced

200 g/7 oz fresh beansprouts

1 red pepper, deseeded and thinly sliced

1 boneless, skin-on cooked chicken breast, about 150 g/ 5½ oz, sliced

12 cooked peeled prawns

1 tbsp groundnut oil

2 tbsp shoyu (Japanese soy sauce)

½ tbsp mirin

1 tsp sesame oil

1 tsp toasted sesame seeds

2 spring onions, finely sliced

NOODLE BASKETS WITH CHICKEN SALAD

SERVES 4

groundnut or corn oil,
  for deep-frying

250 g/9 oz fresh fine or medium
  egg noodles

chicken lime salad

6 tbsp soured cream

6 tbsp mayonnaise

2.5-cm/1-inch piece fresh ginger,
  grated

grated rind and juice of 1 lime

4 skinless, boneless chicken
  thighs, poached and cooled,
  then cut into thin strips

1 carrot, grated

1 cucumber, cut in half
  lengthways, deseeded and
  sliced

1 tbsp finely chopped fresh
  coriander

1 tbsp finely chopped fresh mint

1 tbsp finely chopped fresh
  parsley

salt and pepper

To shape the noodle baskets, you will need a special set of 2 long-handled wire baskets that clip inside each other, available from specialist kitchen stores. Dip the larger wire basket in oil, then line it completely and evenly with one quarter of the noodles. Dip the smaller wire basket in oil, then position it inside the larger basket and clip it into position.

Heat the oil in a wok to 180°C/350°F, or until a cube of bread browns in 30 seconds. Lower the baskets into the oil and deep-fry for 2–3 minutes, or until the noodles are golden brown. Remove the baskets from the oil and drain on kitchen paper. Unclip the 2 wire baskets and carefully remove the small one. Use a palette knife, if necessary, to prise the noodle basket from the wire frame. Repeat to make 3 more baskets. Set aside to cool.

To make the salad, combine the soured cream, mayonnaise, ginger and lime rind. Gradually add the lime juice until you get the flavour you like. Stir in the chicken, carrot and cucumber and season to taste with salt and pepper. Cover and chill.

To serve, stir in the herbs and spoon the salad into the noodle baskets.

TURKEY WITH MUSHROOMS & COURGETTE

Combine all the marinade ingredients in a bowl, then add the turkey and stir. Cover with clingfilm and marinate in the refrigerator for 3–4 hours.

Heat a wok over a high heat, then add the oil. Remove the turkey from the marinade with a slotted spoon, reserving the marinade, and stir-fry a few pieces at a time until browned. Remove the turkey from the wok and set aside.

Add the mushrooms, green pepper and courgette to the wok and stir-fry for 3 minutes. Add the spring onions and stir-fry for a further minute. Add the bamboo shoots and water chestnuts to the wok, then add the turkey and half the reserved marinade. Stir over a medium–high heat for a further 2–3 minutes, until the ingredients are evenly coated and the marinade has reduced.

Serve immediately in warmed dishes with lemon wedges for squeezing over.

SERVES 4

450 g/1 lb turkey breast, cubed

1 tbsp sesame oil

125 g/4½ oz small mushrooms, halved

1 green pepper, deseeded and cut into strips

1 courgette, thinly sliced

4 spring onions, cut into quarters

115 g/4 oz canned bamboo shoots, drained

115 g/4 oz canned water chestnuts, drained and sliced

lemon wedges, to serve

marinade

4 tbsp sweet sherry

1 tbsp lemon juice

1 tbsp soy sauce

2 tsp grated fresh ginger

1 garlic clove, crushed

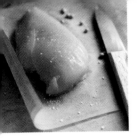

TURKEY TERIYAKI

Mix the glaze ingredients in a small saucepan over low–medium heat. Stir until the honey has melted, then remove from the heat and leave to cool.

Put the turkey in a large shallow dish. Pour over the glaze, turning the strips so they are well coated. Leave to marinate for 30 minutes at room temperature, or overnight in the refrigerator.

Using a slotted spoon, remove the turkey from the marinade, shaking off the excess liquid. Reserve the marinade.

Heat a wok over a medium–high heat, then add the oil. Add the turkey and stir-fry for 2 minutes. Add the yellow pepper and spring onions, and fry for 1 minute. Pour in the reserved marinade. Bring to the boil, then reduce the heat slightly and cook for 3–4 minutes, until the turkey is cooked through.

Transfer the turkey and vegetables to a warmed serving dish. Boil the liquid remaining in the wok until syrupy, then pour over the turkey. Serve immediately with rice.

SERVES 4

450 g/1 lb turkey steaks, cut into strips

3 tbsp groundnut oil

1 small yellow pepper, deseeded and sliced into thin strips

8 spring onions, green part included, diagonally sliced into 2.5-cm/1-inch pieces

freshly cooked plain rice, to serve

teriyaki glaze

5 tbsp shoyu (Japanese soy sauce)

5 tbsp mirin

2 tbsp clear honey

1 tsp finely chopped fresh ginger

TURKEY WITH BOK CHOI & MUSHROOMS

SERVES 4

225 g/8 oz medium egg noodles

3 tbsp groundnut oil

1 large garlic clove, thinly sliced

2 tsp finely chopped fresh ginger

450 g/1 lb turkey steaks, cut into
   thin strips

175 g/6 oz chestnut mushrooms,
   thinly sliced

600 g/1 lb 5 oz bok choi, stalks
   cut into 2.5-cm/1-inch squares
   and leaves sliced into wide
   ribbons

4 spring onions, green part
   included, diagonally sliced into
   2.5-cm/1-inch pieces

1 tbsp light soy sauce

2 tbsp chopped fresh coriander

salt and pepper

Cook the noodles in a saucepan of boiling water for 4 minutes, or according to the instructions on the packet, until soft. Drain, rinse and drain again, then leave to cool.

Heat a wok over a medium–high heat, then add the oil. Stir-fry the garlic and ginger for a few seconds to flavour the oil.

Add the turkey and stir-fry for 2 minutes, until no longer pink. Add the mushrooms and bok choi stalks, and stir-fry for 2 minutes. Add the bok choi leaves and spring onions, and stir-fry for a further 2 minutes. Stir in the noodles and soy sauce, and season to taste with salt and pepper. Cook until the noodles are heated through, then add the coriander. Serve immediately.

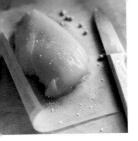

TURKEY WITH HOISIN SAUCE & CASHEW NUTS

To make the marinade, mix the cornflour and rice wine to a paste. Add the pepper, salt, egg white and sesame oil, mixing well. Put the turkey in a shallow dish and add the marinade, turning to coat. Leave to stand for 30 minutes.

Heat a wok over a high heat, then add 3 tablespoons of the groundnut oil. Add the garlic and white spring onion, and stir for a few seconds to flavour the oil. Add the turkey and reduce the heat slightly. Stir-fry for 2 minutes, until no longer pink, then sprinkle with the rice wine. Transfer to a plate with a slotted spoon.

Increase the heat to high and add the remaining groundnut oil. Swirl the oil around the wok, then stir in the hoisin sauce. Return the turkey mixture to the wok and stir-fry for 2–3 minutes, turning to coat, until cooked through.

Add the cashew nuts and green spring onion. Transfer to a warmed serving dish and serve immediately.

SERVES 4

450 g/1 lb turkey steaks, cubed

4 tbsp groundnut oil

3 large garlic cloves, thinly sliced

4 spring onions, white and green parts separated, diagonally sliced into 2-cm/¾-inch pieces

1 tbsp Chinese rice wine or dry sherry

3 tbsp hoisin sauce

4 tbsp cashew nuts

marinade

1 tsp cornflour

1 tbsp Chinese rice wine or dry sherry

¼ tsp white pepper

½ tsp salt

½ egg white, lightly beaten

2 tsp sesame oil

FRUITY DUCK
STIR FRY

Using a sharp knife, cut the duck into thin slices.

Mix the Chinese five-spice and the cornflour. Toss the duck in the mixture until well coated.

Heat a wok over a high heat, then add the oil. Stir-fry the duck for 10 minutes, or until just beginning to crispen around the edges. Remove from the wok and set aside.

Add the onions and garlic to the wok and stir-fry for 5 minutes, or until softened. Add the baby corn and stir-fry for a further 5 minutes. Add the pineapple, spring onions and beansprouts and stir-fry for 3–4 minutes. Stir in the plum sauce.

Return the cooked duck to the wok and toss until well mixed. Transfer to warmed serving dishes and serve hot.

SERVES 4

4 skinless, boneless duck breasts

1 tsp Chinese five-spice

1 tbsp cornflour

1 tbsp chilli oil

225 g/8 oz baby onions, peeled

2 garlic cloves, crushed

100 g/3½ oz baby corn

175 g/6 oz canned pineapple
  chunks

6 spring onions, sliced

100 g/3½ oz fresh beansprouts

2 tbsp plum sauce

THREE-PEA STIR FRY WITH DUCK

SERVES 4

450 g/1 lb skinless, boneless duck breasts

3 tbsp groundnut oil

6 large spring onions, white and green parts separated, diagonally sliced into 2-cm/ ¾-inch pieces

1 tsp finely chopped fresh ginger

175 g/6 oz sugar snap peas

115 g/4 oz mangetout, diagonally sliced in half

140 g/5 oz shelled peas

3 tbsp whole almonds with skin, halved lengthways

55 g/2 oz fresh breansprouts

freshly cooked noodles, to serve

marinade

1 tbsp light brown sugar

3 tbsp warm water

1–2 fresh red chillies, deseeded and very finely chopped

1 tbsp soy sauce

1 tsp Thai fish sauce

3 tbsp lime juice

Combine the marinade ingredients in a bowl, stirring to dissolve the sugar. Slice the duck into bite-sized pieces and add to the marinade. Leave to stand at room temperature for 30 minutes, or overnight in the refrigerator.

Heat a wok over a high heat, then add the oil. Stir-fry the white spring onion and the ginger for a few seconds. Add the duck and the marinade, and stir-fry for about 5 minutes. When the liquid has reduced slightly, add the three types of pea and stir-fry for a further 2–3 minutes.

Add the almonds, beansprouts and green spring onion, and stir-fry for a few seconds to heat through. Serve with noodles.

DUCK WITH MIXED PEPPERS

Heat a wok over a high heat, then add the oil. Cook the duck, skin-side down, for 5–10 minutes, or until crisp and brown. Turn over and cook for a further 5 minutes, until cooked through. Remove the duck from the wok and keep warm.

Pour off any excess fat and stir-fry the onion and garlic for 2–3 minutes, until softened and lightly browned.

Add the peppers and stir-fry for 2–3 minutes, until tender. Add the tomatoes, stock and soy sauce, and simmer for 1–2 minutes. Transfer to a serving plate. Slice the duck thickly and arrange on top, spooning any sauce over it. Serve with noodles.

SERVES 4

1 tbsp vegetable or groundnut oil

2 boneless duck breasts, skin on

1 onion, sliced

2 garlic cloves, chopped

1 red pepper, deseeded and sliced

1 green pepper, deseeded and sliced

1 yellow pepper, deseeded and sliced

4 tomatoes, peeled, deseeded and chopped

150 ml/5 fl oz stock

3 tbsp Thai soy sauce

freshly cooked noodles sprinkled with spring onions, to serve

DUCK WITH BLACK BEANS & BROCCOLI

Remove and discard the skin from the duck. Slice the meat into 5-mm/¼-inch strips.

Soak the beans in cold water for 30 minutes, then drain.

Combine the soy sauce, vinegar and sugar in a small bowl, stirring to dissolve the sugar.

Divide the broccoli into florets. Slice the stems very thinly and slice the florets into pieces no more than 2 cm/¾ inch wide.

Heat a wok over a medium heat, then add the oil. Fry the ginger, chilli and garlic for a few seconds to flavour the oil. Add the drained beans, broccoli and red pepper. Increase the heat to high and stir-fry for 2 minutes.

Add the duck and stir-fry for 2 minutes, then add the soy sauce mixture. Continue to stir-fry for a further 2 minutes. Serve immediately.

SERVES 2–3

2 small duck breasts, weighing 450 g/1 lb in total

2 tbsp salted black beans

1½ tbsp soy sauce

1 tbsp rice vinegar

2 tsp sugar

200 g/7 oz broccoli

3 tbsp groundnut oil

2.5-cm/1-inch piece fresh ginger, cut into very thin shreds

1 fresh red chilli, deseeded and thinly sliced diagonally

1 large garlic clove, thinly sliced

½ red pepper, deseeded and thinly sliced

CANTONESE SWEET & SOUR DUCK

SERVES 6

2 boneless duck breasts, skin on,
  weighing about 550 g/1 lb 4 oz
  in total

½ tbsp soy sauce

2 tsp groundnut oil

salt and pepper

4-cm/1½-inch piece cucumber,
  peeled and sliced lengthways
  into matchsticks, to garnish

sauce

1 tbsp cornflour

125 ml/4 fl oz Basic Chinese Stock
  (see page 16) or chicken stock

1½ tbsp soy sauce

1½ tbsp rice vinegar

2 tbsp sugar

1 tbsp tomato purée

1 tbsp orange juice

2 tsp groundnut oil

3 thin slices fresh ginger

Slice each duck breast into 3 pieces and put in a dish. Rub with salt and pepper and the half tablespoon of soy sauce.

Heat a wok over a medium–high heat, then add the oil. Fry the duck for 6 minutes, starting with the skin side down, and turning until brown and crisp on all sides. Using tongs, transfer to a plate and leave to rest in a warm place for 10 minutes. Discard the oil and wipe the wok clean with kitchen paper. Slice the duck into 1-cm/½-inch strips (the meat will still be quite rare at this stage).

To prepare the sauce, mix the cornflour to a smooth paste with 3 tablespoons of the stock. Combine the soy sauce, vinegar and sugar in a small bowl, stirring to dissolve the sugar. Add the tomato purée and orange juice, mixing well.

Heat the oil in the clean wok over a medium heat. Add the ginger slices and stir-fry for a few seconds to flavour the oil. Add the soy sauce mixture and the remaining stock, and bring to the boil. Reduce the heat slightly and add in the cornflour paste. Stir until starting to thicken, then add the duck slices, stirring to coat with the sauce. Simmer over a low heat for 5 minutes, until the duck is cooked but still slightly pink.

Remove the ginger slices and transfer the duck and sauce to a warmed serving dish. Garnish with the cucumber and serve immediately.

FISH & SEAFOOD

CHILLIES STUFFED WITH FISH PASTE

Combine all the ingredients for the marinade in a bowl and marinate the fish for 20 minutes. Add the egg and mix by hand to create a smooth paste.

To prepare the chillies, cut in half lengthways and scoop out the seeds and loose flesh. Cut into bite-sized pieces. Spread each piece of chilli with about ½ teaspoon of the fish paste.

Heat a wok over a medium–high heat and add the oil. Cook the chilli pieces on both sides until beginning to turn golden brown. Remove from the oil and set aside.

Heat a clean wok over a medium–high heat and add 1 tablespoon of the oil. Stir-fry the garlic until aromatic. Stir in the black beans and mix well. Add the light soy sauce and sugar and stir, then add the chilli pieces. Add the water, then cover and simmer over a low heat for 5 minutes. Serve immediately.

SERVES 4–6

225 g/8 oz white fish, minced

2 tbsp lightly beaten egg

4–6 mild red and green chillies

vegetable or groundnut oil, for shallow-frying

2 garlic cloves, finely chopped

½ tsp fermented black beans, rinsed and lightly mashed

1 tbsp light soy sauce

pinch of sugar

1 tbsp water

marinade

1 tsp finely chopped fresh ginger

pinch of salt

pinch of white pepper

½ tsp vegetable or groundnut oil

FRIED FISH WITH PINE KERNELS

Sprinkle the salt over the fish and set aside for 20 minutes. Squeeze out any excess water from the mushrooms and finely slice, discarding any tough stems.

Heat a wok over a medium–high heat and add 2 tablespoons of the oil. Fry the fish for 3 minutes. Drain and set aside.

Heat a clean wok over a medium–high heat and add the remaining oil. Toss in the ginger. Stir until fragrant, then add the spring onions, peppers, bamboo shoots, mushrooms and Shaoxing and cook for 1–2 minutes.

Finally add the fish and stir to warm through. Sprinkle with the pine kernels and serve.

SERVES 4–6

½ tsp salt

450 g/1 lb thick white fish fillets, cut into 2.5-cm/1-inch cubes

2 dried Chinese mushrooms, soaked in warm water for 20 minutes

3 tbsp vegetable or groundnut oil

2.5-cm/1-inch piece of fresh ginger, finely shredded

1 tbsp chopped spring onions

1 red pepper, deseeded and cut into 2.5-cm/1-inch squares

1 green pepper, deseeded and cut into 2.5-cm/1-inch squares

25 g/1 oz fresh or canned bamboo shoots, rinsed and cut into small cubes (if using fresh shoots, boil in water first for 30 minutes)

2 tsp Shaoxing rice wine

2 tbsp pine kernels, toasted

STIR-FRIED RICE NOODLES WITH MARINATED FISH

SERVES 4

450 g/1 lb monkfish or cod, cubed

225 g/8 oz salmon fillets, cubed

2 tbsp vegetable or groundnut oil

2 fresh green chillies, deseeded
and chopped

grated rind and juice of 1 lime

1 tbsp fish sauce

115 g/4 oz thick rice noodles

2 tbsp vegetable or groundnut oil

2 shallots, sliced

2 garlic cloves, chopped finely

1 fresh red chilli, deseeded and
chopped

2 tbsp Thai soy sauce

2 tbsp chilli sauce

sprigs of fresh coriander,
to garnish

Place the fish in a shallow, non-metallic bowl. To make the marinade, mix together the oil, green chillies, lime juice and rind and fish sauce and pour over the fish. Cover and chill for 2 hours.

Soak the noodles in enough lukewarm water to cover for 15 minutes, or cook according to the instructions on the packet, until soft. Drain well.

Heat a wok over a medium–high heat and add the oil. Sauté the shallots, garlic and red chilli until lightly browned. Add the soy sauce and chilli sauce. Add the fish and the marinade to the wok and stir-fry gently for 2–3 minutes until cooked through.

Add the drained noodles and stir gently. Garnish with coriander and serve immediately.

FISH CURRY WITH RICE NOODLES

Heat a wok over a medium–high heat and add the oil. Gently sauté the onion, garlic and mushrooms until softened but not browned.

Add the fish, curry paste and coconut milk and bring gently to the boil. Simmer for 2–3 minutes, then add half the coriander, the sugar and fish sauce. Keep warm.

Soak the noodles in enough lukewarm water to cover for 15 minutes, or cook according to the instructions on the packet, until soft. Drain well through a colander. Add the spring onions, beansprouts and most of the basil and steam on top of the noodles for 1–2 minutes or until just wilted.

Pile the noodles onto serving plates and top with the fish curry. Sprinkle the remaining coriander and basil over the top and serve immediately.

SERVES 4

2 tbsp vegetable or groundnut oil

1 large onion, chopped

2 garlic cloves, chopped

75 g/3 oz white mushrooms

225 g/8 oz monkfish, cut into cubes, each about 2.5 cm/1 inch

225 g/8 oz salmon fillets, cut into cubes, each about 2.5 cm/1 inch

225 g/8 oz cod, cut into cubes, each about 2.5 cm/1 inch

2 tbsp Thai red curry paste

400 g/14 oz coconut milk

handful of fresh coriander, chopped

1 tsp soft light brown sugar

1 tsp Thai fish sauce

115 g/4 oz medium rice noodles

3 spring onions, chopped

55 g/2 oz fresh beansprouts

few Thai basil leaves

MONKFISH
STIR FRY

Heat a wok over a medium–high heat and add the oil. Add the fish, onion, garlic, ginger, asparagus and mushrooms. Stir-fry for 2–3 minutes.

Stir in the soy sauce and lemon juice and cook for a further minute. Remove from the heat and transfer to serving dishes. Serve immediately.

SERVES 4

2 tsp sesame oil

450 g/1 lb monkfish steaks, cut into 2.5-cm/1-inch chunks

1 onion, thinly sliced

3 garlic cloves, finely chopped

1 tsp grated fresh ginger

225 g/8 oz fine tip asparagus

175 g/6 oz mushrooms, thinly sliced

2 tbsp soy sauce

1 tbsp lemon juice

MONKFISH WITH LIME & CHILLI SAUCE

SERVES 4

4 x 115-g/4-oz monkfish fillets

25 g/1 oz rice flour or cornflour

6 tbsp vegetable or groundnut oil

4 garlic cloves, crushed

2 large fresh red chillies,
   deseeded and sliced

2 tsp soft light brown sugar

juice of 2 limes

grated rind of 1 lime

freshly cooked plain rice, to serve

Toss the fish in the flour, shaking off any excess. Heat a wok over a medium–high heat and add the oil. Cook the fish on all sides until browned and cooked through, taking care when turning not to break it up.

Lift the fish out of the wok and keep warm. Add the garlic and chillies and stir-fry for 1–2 minutes, until they have softened.

Add the sugar, the lime juice and rind and 2–3 tablespoons of water and bring to the boil. Simmer gently for 1–2 minutes, then spoon the mixture over the fish. Serve immediately with rice.

STEAMED SALMON WITH BOK CHOI & ASPARAGUS

Place the salmon steaks in a single layer on a heatproof plate that will fit into a wok. Combine the ginger, wine, soy sauce and salt. Sprinkle this over the fish, rubbing it into the flesh, and leave to stand for 20 minutes, turning once.

Snap the woody ends from the asparagus and discard. Cut off the tips and reserve. Chop the stems into 2 or 3 pieces.

Place a trivet in a wok with a lid, and add enough water to come halfway up the trivet. Bring to the boil, then place the plate of fish on the trivet and cover with a loose tent of foil. Adjust the heat so the water is only just boiling. Put the lid on the wok and steam for 10–15 minutes until the fish is opaque and just starting to flake. Meanwhile, heat a second wok over high heat, then add 2 tablespoons of the groundnut oil. Add the asparagus stalks and bok choi, and stir-fry for 4–5 minutes until just tender but still crisp. Splash with a good squeeze of lime juice and season with salt and pepper. Arrange in small mounds on warm serving plates.

Carefully lift the salmon steaks from the wok and place on top of the vegetables. Heat the sesame oil and remaining groundnut oil until very hot. Add the asparagus tips and stir-fry for 20 seconds until barely cooked. Season with coarsely ground black pepper. Arrange the tips on top of the fish and pour the hot oil over the top. Serve at once with rice.

SERVES 4

4 salmon steaks, about 2.5 cm/1 inch thick

2 tsp finely chopped fresh ginger

2 tbsp Chinese rice wine or dry sherry

1 tbsp light soy sauce

½ tsp salt

8 asparagus spears

4 tbsp groundnut oil

3 heads bok choi, quartered lengthways

good squeeze of lime juice

2 tsp sesame oil

coarsely ground black pepper

freshly cooked plain rice, to serve

SALMON & SCALLOPS WITH CORIANDER & LIME

Heat a wok over a medium–high heat and add the oil. Add the salmon and scallops and stir-fry for 3 minutes. Remove from the wok, set aside and keep warm.

Add the carrots, celery, peppers, mushrooms and garlic to the wok and stir-fry for 3 minutes. Add the coriander and shallots and stir.

Add the lime juice and zest, dried red pepper flakes, sherry and soy sauce and stir. Return the salmon and scallops to the wok and stir-fry carefully for another minute. Serve immediately.

SERVES 4

6 tbsp groundnut oil

280 g/10 oz salmon steak, skinned and cut into 2.5-cm/1-inch chunks

225 g/8 oz scallops

3 carrots, thinly sliced

2 celery stalks, cut into 2.5-cm/1-inch pieces

2 yellow peppers, deseeded and thinly sliced

175 g/6 oz oyster mushrooms, thinly sliced

1 garlic clove, crushed

6 tbsp chopped fresh coriander

3 shallots, thinly sliced

juice of 2 limes

1 tsp lime zest

1 tsp dried red pepper flakes

3 tbsp dry sherry

3 tbsp soy sauce

SAUTÉED MACKEREL FILLETS WITH GINGER & SPRING ONIONS

SERVES 2–3

4 mackerel fillets with skin,
weighing about 450 g in total

1 tsp finely chopped fresh ginger,
plus 2-cm piece finely shredded
lengthways

½ tsp salt

4 tbsp groundnut oil

2½ tbsp plain flour

3 spring onions, green parts
included, sliced

finely shredded Chinese leaves,
to garnish

sauce

2 tbsp light soy sauce

½ tsp sugar

2 tsp Chinese rice wine or dry
sherry

Slice the mackerel fillets in half crossways. Diagonally slash the skin of each piece once or twice. Combine the teaspoon of chopped ginger with the salt. Rub the mixture over both sides of the fish, rubbing it into the slashes and any crevices in the flesh. Leave to stand for 15 minutes.

Combine the sauce ingredients in a small bowl and set aside.

Heat a wok over a medium–high heat and add the oil. Dredge the mackerel fillets in the flour and add to the wok. Fry for 4 minutes, turning once. Pour the sauce over the fish, sprinkle with the shredded ginger and spring onions, and fry for a further 2 minutes.

Transfer to a serving dish and sprinkle with a few shreds of Chinese leaves. Serve at once.

SWEET & SOUR FRIED SWORDFISH

Remove and discard the skin from the fish, and slice into bite-sized chunks. Spread out on a plate and sprinkle with the salt. Sieve the flour and cornflour together to get rid of any lumps, then spread out on a plate.

Next make the sauce. Mix the cornflour, sugar and rice vinegar to a smooth paste. Stir in the soy sauce, tomato purée, cooking wine, orange juice and stock. Heat a wok over a medium–high heat and add the oil. Fry the garlic, ginger and spring onion for 1½ minutes. Add the red and green peppers, and stir-fry for 30 seconds. Pour in the cornflour mixture, increase the heat slightly and stir until thickened. Set aside.

Dip the fish in the beaten egg white, then dredge with the flour-cornflour mixture. Heat a wok, preferably non-stick, over a medium–high heat and add the oil and chicken stock. Add the fish and fry for 5–6 minutes, turning to cook each side. Pour in the sauce and simmer for 1–2 minutes, carefully turning the fish so it is coated with the sauce. Serve.

SERVES 2

450 g/1 lb swordfish steaks

1 tsp salt

4 tsp plain flour

4 tsp cornflour

1 egg white, lightly beaten

1½ tbsp groundnut oil

3 tbsp chicken stock

sweet & sour sauce

2 tsp cornflour

1½ tbsp sugar

1½ tbsp rice vinegar

4 tsp soy sauce

4 tsp tomato purée

4 tsp Chinese rice wine or dry sherry

3 tbsp orange juice

3 tbsp chicken stock

2 tsp vegetable oil

1 large garlic clove, crushed

1 tsp finely chopped fresh ginger

2 tbsp chopped spring onion

¼ small red pepper, deseeded and sliced into thin strips

¼ small green pepper, deseeded and sliced into thin strips

SEAFOOD CHOW MEIN

Open up the squid and score the inside in a criss-cross pattern, then cut into pieces about 2.5 cm/1 inch square. Soak the squid in a bowl of boiling water until all the pieces curl up. Rinse in cold water and drain.

Cut each scallop into 3–4 slices. Cut the prawns in half lengthways if large. Mix the scallops and prawns with the egg white and cornflour paste.

Cook the noodles in a saucepan of boiling water for 4 minutes, or according to the instructions on the packet, until soft. Drain well, then toss with about 1 tablespoon of the oil.

Heat a wok over a medium–high heat and add 3 tablespoons of the oil. Add the noodles and 1 tablespoon of the soy sauce and stir-fry for 2–3 minutes. Remove to a large serving dish.

Heat the remaining oil in the wok and add the mangetout and seafood. Stir-fry for about 2 minutes, then add the salt, sugar, rice wine, the remaining soy sauce and about half the spring onions. Blend well and add a little water if necessary. Pour the seafood mixture on top of the noodles and sprinkle with sesame oil. Garnish with the remaining spring onions and serve immediately.

SERVES 4

85 g/3 oz squid, cleaned

3–4 fresh scallops

85 g/3 oz raw prawns, peeled

½ egg white, lightly beaten

2 tsp cornflour, mixed to a paste with 2½ tsp water

275 g/9¾ oz fine egg noodles

5–6 tbsp vegetable oil

2 tbsp light soy sauce

55 g/2 oz mangetout, sliced diagonally

½ tsp salt

½ tsp sugar

1 tsp Chinese rice wine

2 spring onions, finely shredded

a few drops of sesame oil

SPICY THAI SEAFOOD STEW

SERVES 4

200 g/7 oz squid, cleaned and tentacles discarded

500 g/1 lb 2 oz firm white fish fillet, preferably monkfish or halibut

1 tbsp corn oil

4 shallots, finely chopped

2 garlic cloves, finely chopped

2 tbsp Thai green curry paste

2 small lemon grass stems, finely chopped

1 tsp shrimp paste

500 ml/16 fl oz coconut milk

200 g/7 oz raw king prawns, peeled and deveined

12 live clams in shells, cleaned (see page 248)

8 fresh basil leaves, finely shredded

fresh basil leaves, to garnish

freshly cooked plain rice, to serve

Using a sharp knife, cut the squid body cavities into thick rings and the white fish into bite-size chunks.

Heat a wok over a medium–high heat and add the oil. Add the shallots, garlic and curry paste and stir-fry for 1–2 minutes. Add the lemon grass and shrimp paste, then stir in the coconut milk and bring to the boil.

Reduce the heat until the liquid is simmering gently, then add the white fish, squid and prawns to the wok and simmer for 2 minutes.

Add the clams and simmer for a further 1 minute, or until the clams have opened. Discard any clams that remain closed.

Sprinkle the shredded basil leaves over the stew. Transfer to serving plates, then garnish with whole basil leaves and serve immediately with rice.

MIXED SEAFOOD CURRY

Heat a wok over a medium–high heat and add the oil. Stir-fry the shallots, galangal and garlic for 1–2 minutes, until they start to soften. Add the coconut milk, lemon grass, fish sauce and chilli sauce. Bring to the boil, reduce the heat and simmer for 1–2 minutes.

Add the prawns, squid, salmon and tuna and simmer for 3–4 minutes, until the prawns have turned pink and the fish is cooked.

Add the mussels and cover with a lid. Simmer for 1–2 minutes, until they have opened. Discard any mussels that remain closed. Garnish with Chinese chives and serve immediately with rice.

SERVES 4

1 tbsp vegetable or groundnut oil

3 shallots, chopped finely

2.5-cm/1-inch piece fresh galangal, peeled and sliced thinly

2 garlic cloves, chopped finely

400 ml/14 fl oz canned coconut milk

2 lemon grass stems, snapped in half

4 tbsp Thai fish sauce

2 tbsp chilli sauce

225 g/8 oz uncooked jumbo prawns, shelled

225 g/8 oz baby squid, cleaned and sliced thickly

225 g/8 oz skinned salmon fillet, cut into chunks

175 g/6 oz tuna steak, cut into chunks

225 g/8 oz fresh mussels, scrubbed and debearded

fresh Chinese chives, to garnish

freshly cooked plain rice, to serve

SCALLOPS IN BLACK BEAN SAUCE

Heat a wok over a medium–high heat and add the oil. Add the garlic and stir, then add the ginger and stir-fry together for about 1 minute, until fragrant. Mix in the black beans, add the scallops and stir-fry for 1 minute. Add the light soy sauce, rice wine, sugar and chillies.

Lower the heat and simmer for 2 minutes, then add the stock. Finally add the spring onion, stir and serve.

SERVES 4

2 tbsp vegetable or groundnut oil

1 tsp finely chopped garlic

1 tsp finely chopped fresh ginger

1 tbsp fermented black beans, rinsed and lightly mashed

400 g/14 oz prepared scallops

½ tsp light soy sauce

1 tsp Chinese rice wine

1 tsp sugar

3–4 fresh red bird's-eye chillies, finely chopped

1–2 tsp chicken stock

1 tbsp finely chopped spring onion

SPICY SCALLOPS WITH LIME & CHILLI

SERVES 4

16 large scallops, shelled

1 tbsp butter

1 tbsp vegetable oil

1 tsp crushed garlic

1 tsp grated fresh ginger

1 bunch of spring onions,
   finely sliced

finely grated rind of 1 lime

1 small fresh red chilli, deseeded
   and very finely chopped

3 tbsp lime juice

lime wedges, to garnish

freshly cooked plain rice, to serve

Using a sharp knife, trim the scallops to remove any black intestine, then wash and pat dry with kitchen paper. Separate the corals from the white parts, then slice each white part in half horizontally, making 2 circles.

Heat a wok over a medium heat and add the butter and oil.

Add the garlic and ginger and stir-fry for 1 minute without browning. Add the spring onions and stir-fry for a further 1 minute.

Add the scallops and continue stir-frying over high heat for 4–5 minutes. Stir in the lime rind, chilli and lime juice and cook for a further minute.

Transfer the scallops to serving plates, then spoon over the pan juices and garnish with lime wedges. Serve hot with rice.

CLAMS IN BLACK BEAN SAUCE

Discard any clams with broken shells and any that refuse to close when tapped. Wash the remaining clams thoroughly and leave to soak in clean water until ready to cook.

Heat a wok over a medium–high heat and add the oil. Stir-fry the ginger and garlic until fragrant. Add the black beans and cook for 1 minute.

Over a high heat, add the clams and rice wine and stir-fry for 2 minutes to mix everything together. Cover and cook for a further 3 minutes. Add the spring onion and salt, if necessary, and serve immediately.

SERVES 4

900 g/2 lb small clams

1 tbsp vegetable or groundnut oil

1 tsp finely chopped fresh ginger

1 tsp finely chopped garlic

1 tbsp fermented black beans, rinsed and roughly chopped

2 tsp Chinese rice wine

1 tbsp finely chopped spring onion

1 tsp salt (optional)

STIR-FRIED
FRESH CRAB
WITH GINGER

Heat a wok over a high heat and add 2 tablespoons of the oil.
Cook the crab for 3–4 minutes. Remove and set aside. Wipe the
wok clean.

In the clean wok, heat the remaining oil, then add the ginger
and stir until fragrant. Add the spring onions, then stir in the crab
pieces. Add the soy sauce, sugar and pepper. Cover and simmer
for 1 minute, then serve immediately.

SERVES 4

3 tbsp vegetable or groundnut oil

2 large fresh crabs, cleaned,
 broken into pieces, and legs
 cracked with a cleaver

55 g/2 oz fresh ginger, julienned

100 g/3½ oz spring onions,
 chopped into 5-cm/2-inch
 lengths

2 tbsp light soy sauce

1 tsp sugar

pinch of white pepper

SCALLOP, MANGETOUT & MUSHROOM STIR FRY

SERVES 4

3 tbsp groundnut oil

2 tbsp sesame oil

16 large scallops, halved

225 g/8 oz small shiitake mushrooms, tough stalks removed

175 g/6 oz mangetout, trimmed and halved diagonally

2 tsp finely chopped fresh ginger

2 garlic cloves, finely chopped

2 tsp light soy sauce

juice of 1 lime

3 tbsp torn coriander leaves

salt and pepper

Heat a wok over a high heat and add the oils. Stir-fry the scallops for 1 minute. Add the mushrooms and mangetout, and stir-fry for a further minute.

Add the ginger, garlic and soy sauce, and a splash of water to moisten. Stir-fry for another 1–2 minutes until the vegetables are just tender.

Add the lime juice and coriander leaves, and season to taste. Divide between plates and serve at once.

MALAYSIAN-STYLE COCONUT NOODLES WITH PRAWNS

Heat a wok over a high heat and add the oil. Add the red pepper, bok choi stalks and garlic and stir-fry for 3 minutes. Add the turmeric, garam masala, chilli powder, if using, and bok choi leaves and stir-fry for 1 minute.

Mix the hot stock and peanut butter together in a heatproof bowl until the peanut butter has dissolved, then add to the stir-fry with the coconut milk and soy sauce. Cook for 5 minutes over a medium heat, or until reduced and thickened.

Soak the noodles in enough lukewarm water to cover for 15 minutes, or cook according to the instructions on the packet, until soft. Drain and refresh the noodles under cold running water. Add the cooked noodles and prawns to the coconut curry and cook for a further 2–3 minutes, stirring frequently, until heated through.

Serve the noodle dish sprinkled with spring onions and sesame seeds.

SERVES 4

- 2 tbsp vegetable oil
- 1 small red pepper, deseeded and diced
- 200 g/7 oz bok choi, stalks thinly sliced and leaves chopped
- 2 large garlic cloves, chopped
- 1 tsp ground turmeric
- 2 tsp garam masala
- 1 tsp chilli powder (optional)
- 125 ml/4 fl oz hot vegetable stock
- 2 heaped tbsp smooth peanut butter
- 350 ml/12 fl oz coconut milk
- 1 tbsp soy sauce
- 250 g/9 oz thick rice noodles
- 280 g/10 oz cooked peeled jumbo prawns
- 2 spring onions, finely shredded and 1 tbsp sesame seeds, to garnish

WOK-FRIED KING PRAWNS IN SPICY SAUCE

Heat a wok over a high heat and add the oil. Add the prawns and stir-fry for about 4 minutes, or until just pink. Arrange the prawns on the sides of the wok out of the oil, then add the ginger and garlic and stir until fragrant. Add the spring onion and chilli bean sauce. Stir the prawns into this mixture.

Lower the heat slightly and add the rice wine, sugar, soy sauce and stock. Cover and cook for a further minute. Serve immediately.

SERVES 4

3 tbsp vegetable or groundnut oil

450 g/1 lb raw king prawns, deveined but unpeeled

2 tsp finely chopped fresh ginger

1 tsp finely chopped garlic

1 tbsp chopped spring onion

2 tbsp chilli bean sauce

1 tsp Chinese rice wine

1 tsp sugar

½ tsp light soy sauce

1–2 tbsp chicken stock

PRAWNS FU YUNG

SERVES 4–6

1 tbsp vegetable or groundnut oil

115 g/4 oz large prawns, peeled and deveined

4 eggs, lightly beaten

1 tsp salt

pinch of white pepper

2 tbsp finely chopped Chinese chives

Heat a wok over a high heat and add the oil. Add the prawns and stir-fry for about 4 minutes, or until just pink.

Season the eggs with the salt and pepper and pour over the prawns. Stir-fry for 1 minute, then add the chives.

Cook for a further 4 minutes, stirring all the time, until the eggs are cooked through but still soft in texture. Serve immediately.

PRAWN & PINEAPPLE CURRY

Peel the pineapple and chop the flesh. Heat the coconut cream, pineapple, curry paste, fish sauce and sugar in a wok or saucepan until almost boiling.

Shell and devein the prawns. Add the prawns and chopped coriander to the wok and simmer for 3 minutes, or until the prawns are cooked – they are cooked when they have turned a bright pink colour.

Serve the prawns with jasmine rice.

SERVES 4

½ fresh pineapple

400 ml/14 fl oz coconut cream

2 tbsp Thai red curry paste

2 tbsp fish sauce

2 tsp sugar

350 g/12 oz raw jumbo prawns

2 tbsp chopped coriander

freshly cooked jasmine rice,
  to serve

SWEET CHILLI SQUID

Place the sesame seeds on a baking sheet, toast under a hot grill and set aside.

Heat a wok over a medium heat and add 1 tablespoon of the oil. Add the squid and cook for 2 minutes, then remove and set aside.

Add another 1 tablespoon of the oil to the frying pan and fry the peppers and shallots over a medium heat for 1 minute. Add the mushrooms and fry for a further 2 minutes.

Return the squid to the frying pan and add the sherry, soy sauce, sugar, chilli flakes and garlic, stirring thoroughly. Cook for a further 2 minutes.

Sprinkle with the toasted sesame seeds, drizzle over the remaining sesame oil and mix. Serve on a bed of rice.

SERVES 4

1 tbsp sesame seeds, toasted

2⅓ tbsp sesame oil

280 g/10 oz squid, cut into strips

2 red peppers, deseeded and thinly sliced

3 shallots, thinly sliced

85 g/3 oz mushrooms, thinly sliced

1 tbsp dry sherry

4 tbsp soy sauce

1 tsp sugar

1 tsp hot chilli flakes, or to taste

1 clove of garlic, crushed

freshly cooked plain rice, to serve

TIGER PRAWNS IN TAMARIND SAUCE

SERVES 2

350 g raw headless tiger prawns, unshelled

1½ tbsp finely chopped fresh ginger

2 shallots, finely chopped

½ green chilli, deseeded and finely chopped

groundnut oil, for frying

3 tbsp chopped fresh coriander, to garnish

freshly cooked plain rice, to serve

tamarind sauce

1 tbsp tamarind paste

1 tbsp sugar

2 tsp oyster sauce

2 tbsp water

1 tsp fish sauce

Remove the shells from the prawns leaving the last segment and the tail in place. Combine the ginger, shallots and chilli in a small bowl. Combine the sauce ingredients in another bowl.

Heat a wok over a high heat, then add the oil. When the oil is almost smoking, add the prawns and stir-fry for 3–4 minutes until just pink. Remove from the wok and drain in a colander.

Pour off all but 2 tablespoons of oil from the wok. Heat the remaining oil over a high heat and stir-fry the ginger mixture for 1 minute. Add the tamarind sauce and stir for a few seconds until hot. Add the prawns and stir-fry for 1 minute until the sauce is slightly reduced.

Transfer the prawns to a warm serving dish and sprinkle with the coriander. Serve with rice.

VEGETARIAN

HOT & SOUR COURGETTES

Put the courgette slices in a large colander and toss with the salt. Cover with a plate and put a weight on top. Leave to drain for 20 minutes. Rinse off the salt and spread out the slices on kitchen paper to dry.

Heat a wok over a high heat and add the groundnut oil. Add the Szechuan pepper, chilli, garlic and ginger. Fry for about 20 seconds until the garlic is just beginning to colour.

Add the courgette slices and toss in the oil. Add the rice vinegar, soy sauce and sugar, and stir-fry for 2 minutes. Add the spring onion and fry for 30 seconds. Sprinkle with the sesame oil and seeds, and serve immediately.

SERVES 4

2 large courgettes, thinly sliced

1 tsp salt

2 tbsp groundnut oil

1 tsp Szechuan pepper, crushed

½ –1 red chilli, deseeded and sliced into thin strips

1 large garlic clove, thinly sliced

½ tsp finely chopped fresh ginger

1 tbsp rice vinegar

1 tbsp light soy sauce

2 tsp sugar

1 spring onion, green part included, thinly sliced

a few drops of sesame oil, to garnish

1 tsp sesame seeds, to garnish

AUBERGINE STIR FRY WITH HOT & SOUR SAUCE

First prepare the sauce. Combine the soy sauce, rice vinegar and sugar in a small bowl, stirring to dissolve the sugar. Mix in the cornflour paste and stir until smooth.

Heat the stock and set aside.

Slice the aubergines in half lengthways. With the flat side facing down, slice each half lengthways into 1-cm/½-inch strips. Slice the wider strips lengthways in half again, then cut all the strips crossways into 4-cm/1½-inch pieces.

Heat a wok over a high heat and add 5 tablespoons of the oil. Add the aubergine and red pepper strips and stir-fry for 2–3 minutes until just beginning to colour. Remove from the wok and drain on kitchen paper.

Heat the remaining tablespoon of oil over a high heat. Stir-fry the water chestnuts, spring onions, ginger, garlic and chilli for 1 minute.

Return the aubergine and red pepper to the wok. Reduce the heat to medium, and add soy sauce and the stock. Stir-fry for 2–3 minutes until slightly thickened. Sprinkle with sesame seeds and sliced spring onion tops. Serve with rice.

SERVES 4

- 150 ml/5 fl oz vegetable stock
- 2 aubergines, peeled
- 6 tbsp groundnut oil
- 2 red peppers, deseeded and cut into matchstick strips
- 100 g/3½ oz canned drained water chestnuts, sliced
- 6 spring onions, sliced
- 2 tsp finely chopped fresh ginger
- 1 large garlic clove, thinly sliced
- 1 green chilli, deseeded and finely chopped
- salt and pepper
- 1 tsp sesame seeds and thinly sliced spring onion tops, to garnish
- freshly cooked plain rice, to serve

sauce

- 1½ tbsp soy sauce
- 1½ tbsp rice vinegar
- 2 tsp sugar
- 2 tsp cornflour, blended to a smooth paste with a little water

BROCCOLI WITH PEANUTS

SERVES 4

3 tbsp vegetable or groundnut oil

1 lemon grass stem, roughly chopped

2 fresh red chillies, deseeded and chopped

2.5-cm/1-inch piece fresh ginger, grated

3 kaffir lime leaves, roughly torn

3 tbsp Thai green curry paste

1 onion, chopped

1 red pepper, deseeded and chopped

350 g/12 oz broccoli, cut into florets

115 g/4 oz French beans

55 g/2 oz unsalted peanuts

Put 2 tablespoons of the oil, the lemon grass, chillies, ginger, lime leaves and curry paste into a food processor or blender and process to a paste.

Heat a wok over a medium heat and add the remaining oil. Add the spice paste, onion and red pepper and stir-fry for 2–3 minutes, until the vegetables start to soften.

Add the broccoli and French beans, cover and cook over a low heat, stirring occasionally, for 4–5 minutes, until tender.

Meanwhile, toast or dry-fry the peanuts until lightly browned. Add them to the broccoli mixture and toss together. Serve immediately.

VEGETARIAN

273

MUSHROOMS & FRENCH BEANS WITH LEMON & CORIANDER

Rinse the mushrooms and dry with kitchen paper. If using clumping mushrooms, such as enoki and buna shimeji, slice off the root and separate the clump. Slice cremini mushrooms in half.

Heat a wok over a medium–high heat and add the oil. Add the coriander seeds and bay leaf, and fry for a few seconds to flavour the oil. Add the mushrooms and beans, and stir-fry for 5 minutes.

Stir in the garlic, lemon juice and soy sauce. Season with salt and freshly ground black pepper, and stir-fry for 2 minutes. Sprinkle with the coriander, sesame oil and seeds, and fry for a few seconds. Serve hot, warm or at room temperature.

SERVES 2

450 g/1 lb mixed small mushrooms such as cremini, enoki and buna shimeji

6 tbsp rapeseed oil

1 tsp coriander seeds, crushed

1 fresh bay leaf

175 g/6 oz French beans

1 large garlic clove, thinly sliced

3 tbsp lemon juice

2 tsp soy sauce

2 tbsp chopped coriander

2 tsp sesame oil

2 tsp sesame seeds

salt and pepper

SPICY TOFU
WITH RICE

Combine all the marinade ingredients in a bowl. Add the tofu and toss well to cover in the marinade. Set aside to marinate for 20 minutes.

Heat a wok over a medium–high heat and add 2 tablespoons of the oil. Stir-fry the tofu with its marinade until brown and crispy. Remove from the wok and set aside.

Heat the remaining 2 tablespoons of oil in the wok and stir-fry the ginger, garlic and spring onions for 30 seconds. Add the broccoli, carrot, yellow pepper and mushrooms and cook for 5–6 minutes. Return the tofu to the wok and stir-fry to reheat. Serve immediately with rice.

SERVES 6

250 g/9 oz firm tofu, rinsed, drained and cut into 1-cm/½-inch cubes

4 tbsp groundnut oil

1 tbsp grated fresh ginger

3 garlic cloves, crushed

4 spring onions, thinly sliced

1 head of broccoli, cut into florets

1 carrot, cut into batons

1 yellow pepper, deseeded and thinly sliced

250 g/9 oz shiitake mushrooms, thinly sliced

freshly cooked plain rice, to serve

marinade

5 tbsp vegetable stock

2 tsp cornflour

2 tbsp light soy sauce

1 tbsp caster sugar

pinch of chilli flakes

AGEDASHI TOFU

SERVES 2

150 ml/5 fl oz water

2 tsp dashi granules

2 tbsp shoyu (Japanese soy sauce)

2 tbsp mirin

vegetable oil, for deep-frying

300 g/10½ oz silken tofu, drained on kitchen paper and cut into 4 cubes

2 tbsp plain flour

to garnish

1 tsp grated fresh ginger

2 tsp grated daikon

¼ tsp kezuri-bushi shavings

Put the water in a pan with the dashi granules and bring to the boil. Add the shoyu and mirin and cook for 1 minute. Keep warm.

Heat a large wok over a high heat. Pour in the oil and heat to 180°C/350°F or until a cube of bread browns in 30 seconds. Meanwhile, dust the tofu cubes with the flour.

Add the tofu pieces to the oil, in batches, and cook until lightly golden in colour. Remove, drain on kitchen paper and keep hot while you cook the remaining tofu cubes.

Put 2 pieces of tofu in each of 2 bowls and divide the dashi stock between them. Garnish with ginger, daikon and kezuri-bushi.

OYSTER MUSHROOMS & VEGETABLES WITH PEANUT CHILLI SAUCE

Heat a wok over a high heat, add the oil and heat until almost smoking. Stir-fry the spring onions for 1 minute. Add the carrot and courgette and stir-fry for another minute. Then add the broccoli and cook for a further minute.

Stir in the mushrooms and cook until they are soft and at least half the liquid they produce has evaporated. Add the peanut butter and stir well, then season with the chilli powder to taste. Finally add the water and cook for 1 minute.

Garnish with lime wedges and serve with rice.

SERVES 6

1 tbsp vegetable or groundnut oil

4 spring onions, finely sliced

1 carrot, cut into thin strips

1 courgette, cut into thin strips

½ head of broccoli, cut into florets

450 g/1 lb oyster mushrooms, thinly sliced

2 tbsp crunchy peanut butter

1 tsp chilli powder, or to taste

3 tbsp water

lime wedges, to garnish

freshly cooked plain rice, to serve

SWEET & SOUR VEGETABLES ON NOODLE PANCAKES

Soak the noodles in enough lukewarm water to cover for 15 minutes, or cook according to the instructions on the packet, until soft. Drain well and use scissors to cut them into 7.5-cm/ 3-inch lengths.

Meanwhile, prepare the vegetables as necessary.

Beat the eggs, then stir in the noodles, spring onions, salt and pepper. Heat a 20-cm/8-inch frying pan over a high heat. Add 1 tablespoon of the oil and swirl it around. Pour in a quarter of the egg mixture and tilt the frying pan so it covers the bottom. Lower the heat to medium and cook for 1 minute, or until the thin pancake is set. Flip it over and add a little extra oil, if necessary. Continue cooking until beginning to colour. Transfer to a plate and keep warm in a low oven while you make 3 more pancakes.

When you have made 4 pancakes, heat a wok over a high heat and add the remaining oil. Add the thickest vegetables, such as carrots, first and stir-fry for 30 seconds. Gradually add the remaining vegetables and the bamboo shoots. Stir in the sauce and stir-fry until all the vegetables are tender and the sauce is hot. Spoon the vegetables and sauce over the pancakes.

SERVES 4

115 g/4 oz fine rice noodles

900 g/2 lb selection of vegetables, such as carrots, baby corn, cauliflower, broccoli, mangetout, mushrooms and onions, peeled as necessary and chopped into equal-sized pieces

6 eggs

4 spring onions, sliced diagonally

2½ tbsp vegetable or groundnut oil

100 g/3½ oz canned bamboo shoots, drained

200 ml/7 fl oz sweet and sour sauce

salt and pepper

ASIAN VEGETABLES WITH YELLOW BEAN SAUCE

SERVES 4

1 aubergine

salt

2 tbsp vegetable oil

3 garlic cloves, crushed

4 spring onions, chopped

1 small red pepper, deseeded and
    thinly sliced

4 baby corn, halved lengthways

115 g/4 oz mangetout

200 g/7 oz green bok choi,
    coarsely shredded

425 g/14½ oz canned straw
    mushrooms, drained

115 g/4 oz fresh beansprouts

2 tbsp Chinese rice wine or
    dry sherry

2 tbsp yellow bean sauce

2 tbsp dark soy sauce

1 tsp chilli sauce

1 tsp sugar

150 ml/5 fl oz vegetable stock

1 tsp cornflour

2 tsp water

Cut the aubergine into 5-cm/2-inch-long thin sticks. Place in a colander, then sprinkle with salt and let stand for 30 minutes. Rinse in cold water and dry thoroughly with kitchen paper.

Heat a wok over a medium–high heat and add the oil. Add the garlic, spring onions and pepper and stir-fry over a high heat for 1 minute. Stir in the aubergine pieces and stir-fry for a further minute, or until softened.

Stir in the baby corn and mangetout and stir-fry for 1 minute. Add the bok choi, mushrooms and beansprouts and stir-fry for 30 seconds.

Mix the rice wine, yellow bean sauce, soy sauce, chilli sauce and sugar together in a bowl, then add to the pan with the stock. Bring to the boil, stirring constantly.

Slowly blend the cornflour with the water to form a smooth paste, then stir quickly into the pan and cook for a further minute. Serve immediately.

CHINESE VEGETABLES & BEANSPROUTS WITH NOODLES

Heat a wok over a medium–high heat and bring the stock, ginger and garlic to the boil. Stir in the noodles, red pepper, peas, broccoli and mushrooms and return to the boil. Reduce the heat, cover and simmer for 5–6 minutes, or until the noodles are tender.

Meanwhile, preheat the grill to medium. Spread the sesame seeds out in a single layer on a baking sheet and toast under the preheated grill, turning to brown evenly – watch constantly because they brown very quickly. Tip the sesame seeds into a small dish and set aside.

Once the noodles are tender, add the water chestnuts, bamboo shoots, Napa cabbage, beansprouts and spring onions to the wok. Return the stock to the boil, stir to mix the ingredients and simmer for a further 2–3 minutes to heat through thoroughly.

Carefully drain off 300 ml/10 fl oz of the stock into a small heatproof jug and set aside. Drain and discard any remaining stock and turn the noodles and vegetables into a serving dish. Quickly mix the soy sauce with the reserved stock and pour over the noodles and vegetables. Season with pepper and serve at once.

SERVES 4

1.25 litres/40 fl oz vegetable stock

1 garlic clove, crushed

1-cm/½-inch piece fresh ginger, finely chopped

225 g/8 oz medium egg noodles

1 red pepper, deseeded and sliced

85 g/3 oz frozen peas

115 g/4 oz broccoli florets

85 g/3 oz shiitake mushrooms, sliced

2 tbsp sesame seeds

225 g/8 oz canned water chestnuts, drained and halved

225 g/8 oz canned bamboo shoots, drained

280 g/10 oz Napa cabbage, sliced

140 g/5 oz fresh beansprouts

3 spring onions, sliced

1 tbsp dark soy sauce

pepper

CRISP NOODLE & VEGETABLE STIR FRY

Heat a large wok over a high heat. Pour in the oil and heat to 180°C/350°F or until a cube of bread browns in 30 seconds.

Add the noodles, in batches, and cook for 1½–2 minutes, or until crisp and puffed up. Remove and drain on kitchen paper. Pour off all but 2 tablespoons of oil from the wok.

Heat the remaining oil over high heat. Add the French beans and stir-fry for 2 minutes. Add the carrot and courgette sticks, sliced mushrooms and ginger and stir-fry for a further 2 minutes.

Add the shredded Napa cabbage, spring onions and beansprouts and stir-fry for a further minute. Add the soy sauce, rice wine and sugar and cook, stirring constantly, for 1 minute.

Add the chopped coriander and toss well. Serve immediately, with the noodles.

SERVES 4

peanut or sunflower oil,
   for deep-frying

115 g/4 oz rice vermicelli, broken
   into 7.5-cm/3-inch lengths

115 g/4 oz French beans,
   cut into short lengths

2 carrots, cut into thin sticks

2 courgettes, cut into thin sticks

115 g/4 oz shiitake mushrooms,
   sliced

2.5-cm/1-inch piece fresh ginger,
   shredded

½ small head Napa cabbage,
   shredded

4 spring onions, shredded

85 g/3 oz fresh beansprouts

2 tbsp dark soy sauce

2 tbsp Chinese rice wine

large pinch of sugar

2 tbsp coarsely chopped fresh
   coriander

SPICY NOODLES WITH MUSHROOM EGG ROLLS

SERVES 4

2 tbsp vegetable or groundnut oil

1 small onion, chopped finely

225 g/8 oz mushrooms, chopped

1 tbsp Thai red curry paste

1 tbsp Thai soy sauce

8 square egg roll skins

vegetable or groundnut oil,
  for deep-frying

225 g/8 oz quick-cook noodles

1 garlic clove, chopped

6 spring onions, chopped

1 red pepper, deseeded and
  chopped

1 tbsp ground coriander

1 tbsp ground cumin

Heat a wok over a medium–high heat and add 1 tablespoon of the oil. Stir-fry the onion and mushrooms until crisp and browned. Add the curry paste and soy sauce and stir-fry for 2–3 minutes. Remove the wok from the heat.

Spoon an eighth of the mixture across one of the egg roll skins and roll up, folding the sides over the filling to enclose it.

Clean the wok and heat over a high heat. Pour in the oil and heat to 180°C/350°F or until a cube of bread browns in 30 seconds. Deep-fry the egg rolls, 4 at a time, until crisp and browned. Drain on kitchen paper and keep warm.

Meanwhile, put the noodles in a bowl, cover with boiling water and set aside to swell.

Heat the remaining oil in the wok and stir-fry the garlic, spring onions and red pepper for 2–3 minutes. Stir in the coriander and cumin, then drain the noodles and add them to the wok. Toss together and serve topped with the egg rolls.

MUSHROOM & TOFU LAKSA WITH NOODLES

Purée the spice paste ingredients in a food processor, pulsing several times until smooth.

Heat a wok over a medium–high heat, add the spice paste and stir-fry for 30 seconds. Pour in the stock and coconut milk, and bring to the boil. Add the mushrooms, tofu and tomato purée and season with salt and freshly ground black pepper. Simmer gently for 5 minutes.

Cook the noodles in a saucepan of boiling water for 4 minutes, or according to the instructions on the packet, until soft. Divide between four large soup bowls. Ladle the spicy broth over the noodles. Serve with the garnishes.

SERVES 4

850 ml/1½ pints vegetable stock

400 g/14 oz canned coconut milk

250 g/9 oz shiitake mushrooms, stalks removed, thinly sliced

150 g/5¼ oz firm tofu, cubed

2 tbsp tomato purée

175 g/6 oz fine egg noodles

salt and pepper

8 spring onions, sliced, and 4 tbsp shredded mint leaves, to garnish

spice paste

2 red chillies, deseeded and chopped

4 cm/1½ inch piece fresh ginger, chopped

2 large garlic cloves, chopped

2 lemon grass stems, tough outer layers discarded, inner stalks chopped

1 tsp coriander seeds, crushed

6 macadamia nuts, chopped

small handful of coriander leaves

3 tbsp vegetable oil

SZECHUAN NOODLES

Peel the carrot and cut off both ends, then grate it lengthways on the coarsest side of a grater to make long, thin strips. Set the carrot strips aside.

Cook the noodles in a saucepan of boiling water for 4 minutes, or according to the instructions on the packet, until soft. Drain and rinse with cold water to stop the cooking, then set aside.

Heat a wok over a high heat and add the oil. Add the garlic and onion and stir-fry for 1 minute. Add the vegetable stock, chilli bean sauce, sesame paste, ground Szechuan peppercorns and soy sauce and bring to the boil, stirring to blend the ingredients together. Add the bok choi quarters and carrot strips and continue stir-frying for 1–2 minutes, until they are just wilted. Add the noodles and continue stir-frying, using 2 forks to mix all the ingredients together until the noodles are hot, then serve.

SERVES 4

1 large carrot

250 g/9 oz thick egg noodles

2 tbsp peanut or corn oil

2 large garlic cloves, very finely chopped

1 large red onion, cut in half and thinly sliced

125 ml/4 fl oz vegetable stock or water

2 tbsp bottled chilli bean sauce

2 tbsp Chinese sesame paste

1 tbsp dried Szechuan peppercorns, roasted and ground

1 tsp light soy sauce

2 small bok choi or other Chinese cabbage, cut into quarters

BROCCOLI & MANGETOUT STIR FRY

SERVES 4

2 tbsp vegetable or groundnut oil

dash of sesame oil

1 garlic clove, finely chopped

225 g/8 oz small head of broccoli, broken into florets

115 g/4 oz mangetout

225 g/8 oz Chinese leaves, chopped into 1-cm/½-inch slices

5–6 spring onions, finely chopped

½ tsp salt

2 tbsp light soy sauce

1 tbsp Chinese rice wine

1 tsp sesame seeds, lightly toasted, to garnish

Heat a wok over a medium–high heat and add the oils. Add the garlic and stir-fry vigorously. Add all the vegetables and salt and stir-fry over a high heat, tossing rapidly, for about 3 minutes.

Pour in the soy sauce and rice wine and cook for a further 2 minutes. Sprinkle with the sesame seeds and serve hot.

GARLIC
SPINACH
STIR FRY

Heat a wok over a high heat and add the oil. Add the garlic, black bean sauce and tomatoes and stir-fry for 1 minute.

Stir in the spinach, chilli sauce and lemon juice and mix well. Cook, stirring frequently, for 3 minutes, or until the spinach is just wilted. Season with salt and pepper. Remove from the heat and serve immediately.

SERVES 4

6 tbsp vegetable oil

6 garlic cloves, crushed

2 tbsp black bean sauce

3 tomatoes, roughly chopped

900 g/2 lb spinach, tough stalks
   removed, roughly chopped

1 tsp chilli sauce, or to taste

2 tbsp fresh lemon juice

salt and pepper

SPICY VEGETARIAN STIR FRY

Heat a wok over a medium–high heat and add 2 tablespoons of the oil. Add the turmeric and a pinch of salt. Carefully add the potatoes, stirring continuously to coat in the turmeric. Stir-fry for 5 minutes, then remove from the wok and set aside.

Heat the remaining tablespoon of oil and stir-fry the shallots for 1–2 minutes. Mix in the bay leaf, cumin, ginger and chilli powder, then add the tomatoes and stir-fry for 2 minutes.

Add the spinach, mixing well to combine all the flavours. Cover and simmer for 2–3 minutes. Return the potatoes to the wok and add the peas and lemon juice. Cook for 5 minutes, or until the potatoes are tender.

Remove the wok from the heat and discard the bay leaf, then season with salt and pepper. Serve with basmati rice.

SERVES 4

3 tbsp vegetable oil

½ tsp turmeric

225 g/8 oz potatoes, cut into 1-cm/½-inch cubes

3 shallots, finely chopped

1 bay leaf

½ tsp ground cumin

1 tsp finely grated fresh ginger

¼ tsp chilli powder

4 tomatoes, coarsely chopped

spinach, tough stalks removed, roughly chopped

125 g/4½ oz fresh or frozen peas

1 tbsp lemon juice

freshly cooked basmati rice, to serve

salt and pepper

RED CURRY WITH MIXED LEAVES

SERVES 4

2 tbsp groundnut or vegetable oil

2 onions, thinly sliced

1 bunch of fine asparagus spears

400 ml/14 fl oz coconut milk

2 tbsp Thai red curry paste

3 fresh kaffir lime leaves

225 g/8 oz baby spinach leaves

2 heads bok choi, chopped

1 small head Chinese leaves, shredded

handful of fresh coriander, chopped

freshly cooked plain rice, to serve

Heat a wok over a medium–high heat and add the oil. Add the onions and asparagus and stir-fry for 1–2 minutes.

Add the coconut milk, curry paste and lime leaves and bring gently to the boil, stirring occasionally. Add the spinach, bok choi and Chinese leaves and cook, stirring, for 2–3 minutes, until wilted. Add the coriander and stir well. Serve immediately with rice.

CARROT & PUMPKIN CURRY

Pour the stock into a large saucepan and bring to the boil. Add the galangal, half the garlic, the lemon grass and chillies and simmer for 5 minutes. Add the carrots and pumpkin and simmer for 5–6 minutes, until tender.

Heat a wok over a medium–high heat and add the oil. Stir-fry the shallots and the remaining garlic for 2–3 minutes. Add the curry paste and stir-fry for 1–2 minutes.

Stir the shallot mixture into the saucepan and add the coconut milk and Thai basil. Simmer for 2–3 minutes. Serve hot, sprinkled with the toasted pumpkin seeds.

SERVES 4

150 ml/5 fl oz vegetable stock

2.5-cm/1-inch piece fresh galangal, sliced

2 garlic cloves, chopped

1 lemon grass stem (white part only), finely chopped

2 fresh red chillies, deseeded and chopped

4 carrots, peeled and cut into chunks

225 g/8 oz pumpkin, peeled, deseeded and cut into cubes

2 tbsp vegetable or groundnut oil

2 shallots, finely chopped

3 tbsp Thai yellow curry paste

400 ml/14 fl oz coconut milk

4–6 fresh Thai basil sprigs

25 g/1 oz toasted pumpkin seeds, to garnish

CABBAGE & COCONUT CURRY

Purée the spice paste ingredients in a food processor or blender, adding a splash of water to moisten.

Heat a wok over a medium–high heat and add the oil. Fry the mustard seeds until they start to crackle. Reduce the heat to medium, then add the onion and stir-fry until golden. Stir in the spice paste and fry for 30 seconds.

Add the shredded white and green cabbage and pour in the water, stirring well so the cabbage is covered with the paste. Season with the crushed peppercorns and a little salt. Cover and cook over low heat for 7–10 minutes, stirring now and again to prevent sticking.

When the cabbage is tender, add the coconut flakes, coriander and lime juice. Stir for a minute to heat through and serve.

SERVES 4–6

3 tbsp vegetable oil

1 tsp mustard seeds

1 small onion sliced

¼ white cabbage, core removed, leaves shredded

½ small green cabbage, core removed, leaves shredded

100–125 ml/3–4 fl oz water

½ tsp black peppercorns, crushed

4 tbsp toasted coconut flakes

3 tbsp chopped coriander leaves

juice of ½ lime

salt

spice paste

50 g sachet creamed coconut, melted

1 green chilli, deseeded and roughly chopped

1 tbsp finely chopped fresh ginger

2 garlic cloves, sliced

1 small onion, finely chopped

½ tsp salt

1 tsp cumin seeds

½ tsp ground turmeric

AUBERGINE & BEAN CURRY

SERVES 4

2 tbsp vegetable or groundnut oil

1 onion, chopped

2 garlic cloves, crushed

2 fresh red chillies, deseeded and chopped

1 tbsp Thai red curry paste

1 large aubergine, cut into chunks

115 g/4 oz small aubergines

115 g/4 oz baby broad beans

115 g/4 oz French beans

300 ml/10 fl oz vegetable stock

55 g/2 oz block creamed coconut, chopped

3 tbsp Thai soy sauce

1 tsp soft light brown sugar

3 kaffir lime leaves, torn coarsely

4 tbsp chopped fresh coriander

Heat a wok over a medium–high heat and add the oil. Sauté the onion, garlic and chillies for 1–2 minutes. Stir in the curry paste and cook for 1–2 minutes.

Add the aubergines and cook for 3–4 minutes, until starting to soften. (You may need to add a little more oil as aubergines soak it up quickly.) Add the beans and stir-fry for 2 minutes.

Pour in the stock and add the creamed coconut, soy sauce, sugar and lime leaves. Bring gently to the boil and cook until the coconut has dissolved. Stir in the coriander and serve hot.

VEGETARIAN

309

COURGETTE & CASHEW NUT CURRY

Heat a wok over a medium–high heat and add the oil. Sauté the onions, garlic and chillies for 1–2 minutes, until softened but not browned.

Add the courgettes and mushrooms to the wok and cook for 2–3 minutes until tender.

Add the beansprouts, nuts, chives and soy sauce and stir-fry for 1–2 minutes.

Serve hot with rice or noodles.

SERVES 4

2 tbsp vegetable or groundnut oil

6 spring onions, chopped

2 garlic cloves, chopped

2 fresh green chillies, deseeded and chopped

450 g/1 lb courgettes, cut into thick slices

115 g/4 oz shiitake mushrooms, halved

55 g/2 oz fresh beansprouts

75 g/3 oz cashew nuts, toasted or dry-fried

few Chinese chives, chopped

4 tbsp Thai soy sauce

freshly cooked plain rice or noodles, to serve

EGG FRIED RICE WITH VEGETABLES & CRISPY ONIONS

Heat a wok over a medium–high heat and add half the oil. Sauté the garlic and chillies for 2–3 minutes.

Add the mushrooms, mangetout and baby corn and stir-fry for 2–3 minutes, then add the soy sauce, sugar and basil. Stir in the rice.

Push the mixture to one side of the wok and add the eggs to the bottom. Stir until lightly set before combining into the rice mixture.

Heat the remaining oil in another pan and sauté the onions until crispy and brown. Serve the rice topped with the onions and garnished with Thai basil leaves.

SERVES 4

4 tbsp vegetable or groundnut oil

2 garlic cloves, chopped finely

2 fresh red chillies, deseeded and chopped

115 g/4 oz mushrooms, sliced

55 g/2 oz mangetout, halved

55 g/2 oz baby corn, halved

3 tbsp Thai soy sauce

1 tbsp soft light brown sugar

few Thai basil leaves, plus extra to garnish

350 g/12 oz rice, cooked and cooled

2 eggs, beaten

2 onions, sliced

EGG FU YUNG

SERVES 4–6

2 eggs

½ tsp salt

pinch of white pepper

1 tsp melted butter

2 tbsp vegetable or groundnut oil

1 tsp finely chopped garlic

1 small onion, finely sliced

1 green pepper, deseeded and
   finely sliced

450 g/1 lb cooked rice, chilled

1 tbsp light soy sauce

1 tbsp finely chopped spring
   onions

150 g/5 oz fresh beansprouts,
   trimmed

2 drops of sesame oil

Beat the eggs with the salt and pepper. Heat the butter in a frying pan and pour in the eggs. Cook as an omelette, until set, then remove from the pan and cut into slivers.

Heat a wok over a medium–high heat and add the oil. Stir-fry the garlic until fragrant. Add the onion and stir-fry for 1 minute, then add the green pepper and stir-fry for a further 1 minute. Stir in the rice and, when the grains are separated, stir in the light soy sauce and cook for 1 minute.

Add the spring onions and egg strips and stir well, then add the beansprouts and sesame oil. Stir-fry for 1 minute and serve.

INDEX

INDEX